grace!

un Duly

Eph 2:8

Grace Changes
Everything

The Truth That Sets Us Free.....

Kevin Derby

WestBow
PRESS
A DIVISION OF THOMAS NELSON

ISBN: 978-1-4497-5539-3 (sc)
ISBN: 978-1-4497-5540-9 (hc)
ISBN: 978-1-4497-5538-6 (e)

Library of Congress Control Number: 2012910192

WestBow Press books may be ordered through booksellers or by contacting:

WestBow Press
A Division of Thomas Nelson
1663 Liberty Drive
Bloomington, IN 47403
www.westbowpress.com
1-(866) 928-1240

Printed in the United States of America

WestBow Press rev. date: 09/11/2012

Many Thanks to:

Mark and Kathy Levesque. You shared a message that changed my life forever!

Rick and Jamie Dement: My spiritual mentors, true examples of Christ.

My parents. You guys hung in there with me through it all, and prayed for me when I couldn't pray for myself.

My sons, Kevin and Josh. Two boys who have grown into Godly men. I'm proud of you both.

My Uncle Gene and Aunt Betty. You started this whole thing almost 40 years ago when you asked me if I wanted to know Jesus.

My grandparents. They are with the Lord now, but they left so much behind here for me, that words can't express my love and adoration for them both.

The pastoral staff, directors, leaders and those who call Discovery Church home. Your lives are a true reflection of God's grace.

To Pat, Kathy and Janet for editing this book.

Shirley, My wife and best friend. You of all people know the whole story and are taking this journey with me. I love you and thank God for you.

God. Your grace changes everything.

Table of Contents

Introduction

What is your understanding of grace? How have you seen grace modeled? Have you ever experienced true grace? Is God's grace unconditional? How *should* grace affect your relationship with God and others?

I remember attending church as a child and "accepting" Jesus, but life never really changed. The message of Jesus impacted me during Sunday service, but by midweek, things seemed to return to the way they were. I couldn't grasp how "all things had become new" when, from my vantage point, nothing had changed. Especially me! No matter how much I tried I couldn't get it! But I pressed on. If nothing else I would fake it, until I made it.

At a crucial point in my teenage years, family tragedy struck. During this time I tried to find comfort in God. I prayed, read the Bible and went to church every time the doors were open. Nothing helped. I thought if life was this bad with Jesus, what's the use? I believed in Him and figured that would be enough to ensure I would go to heaven. After all, wasn't that the end goal in this whole Christian thing?

For many, this story is all too familiar. They desperately want things to be different in their lives, even to the point of "getting saved." But after the newness wears off they are right back where they started.

Years after walking away from church, I began attending church again. A few years later I entered the ministry, convinced my relationship with Jesus could be patched up. I knew from an early age that God had "called" me (actually, God calls everybody) into the ministry and it was time to "follow" that call. But once again, after the newness had worn off, I experienced the same spiritual dryness and ambiguity that had plagued me previously. Convinced this was just how life as a believer would be, I pressed on. After all, wasn't Jesus a man acquainted with sorrow? Unfortunately, after a few years of "pressing on," that dryness overtook me and became too much to bear. I left the ministry and resigned myself to the fact that I didn't have what it took to be a pastor. Enter grace!

After a year of feeling sorry for myself and floundering through life, I decided that even if I couldn't serve in the capacity I wanted, staying away from other believers wasn't the answer. Not long after my return to church life, I became aware of problems within the church I attended. The church was in crisis and there was work to be done. I was asked by the leadership if I would pray about stepping into an elder position. Honestly, I didn't want anything to do with church leadership. I remembered the pain of past experiences while serving in church leadership and the wounds were still fresh. I had reached a crossroads. I didn't know what to do, but running wasn't the answer. God reaffirmed this during my times of prayer.

> For God hath not given us the spirit of fear; but of
> power, and of love, and of a sound mind.
> 2 Timothy 1:7 KJV

Those words were written by the apostle Paul to encourage a young pastor to stay the course. Those words were written by Paul as he shared the grace-filled message of Jesus Christ. Those words were for me.

Through this crisis, God began to teach me about His power and His grace. I would get telephone calls from people who had no idea of what was happening with the leadership, and they would say things like, "God wants me to tell you to stay strong." I continued to receive call after call, encouraging me, even though these people had no idea of what was taking place in the church.

For the first time in my Christian life, I heard from people who said that "God told them" about me and what was going on in my life. These were things they couldn't know, things only I and a few close tight-lipped people in leadership knew at that time.

It was during this time that my relationship with Mark, one of the church elders, began to stretch my understanding of God and His grace. Mark and I had served as elders on the leadership team for a short time, and during this time, I had developed a deep respect for Mark. His life reflected his beliefs.

During this time of transition within the church, the pastors' wives had begun to meet once a week. After one of these meetings, my wife came home and shared with me a conversation about sin that had taken place. Mark's wife, Kathy, had made a statement during Bible study that didn't make any sense. Her point was that while knowing we are sinners is the problem, realizing our righteousness is the answer.

> But God commendeth his love toward us, in that, while we were yet sinners, Christ died for us.
> Romans 5:8 KJV

The apostle Paul said, "While we *were* yet sinners.

At first I dismissed this statement as "over the top," but from that single statement, God began to lead me deep into the Scriptures. I began to read the Bible from a completely different perspective. From past teachings and self-study I knew what the Bible said about who we were in His eyes, but a more complete understanding of what God actually meant began to settle in my spirit. The journey had begun.

Mark and I spent many hours laughing together about this new revelation of grace. It was something Mark had experienced many years earlier but was reluctant to share with others.

Mark recalled how he would often try to share from the Bible God's message of grace which often met with contention from many church leaders. When his wife Kathy "spilled the beans," his first thought was "here we go again!" But that wasn't the case. In fact, it was just the opposite. People began to walk in freedom. I began to live in freedom. I remember telling Mark, "It feels like I have been born again, again!" I am deeply indebted to Mark and Kathy and thank God they were willing to step out in faith to share a message that has changed my life.

With a new revelation of God's grace, I began to look back at my life. I realized how God had been there all along, watching and waiting for me. The words on the pages of the Bible came alive. All the promises and power of God I read about in the Bible were not only records of God's past glory, but also promises of present grace and power to His people today. These accounts of other people of the Bible became my story. His promises were for me.

But God is not a bully. He won't force His love on us, no matter how much He knows we need it. I know, in retrospect, God was always there, just as he promised, even in the middle of my chaotic life.

We probably all have stories from our past that show us in the present how God has always been there waiting for us. An experience I had while serving in the military brought this point home to me in a real and personal way.

A year after I graduated from high school, I enlisted in the Air Force. My first duty station was Tyndall Air Force Base near Panama City Beach in Florida. My weekends were usually spent partying on the white sands while listening to music, lifting weights and getting an awesome tan. During one of those weekends a friend named José decided to swim out to a sand bar about 150 yards off the beach. I knew that wasn't a good idea, having grown up in Florida and knowing that riptides, ocean currents and heavy drinking don't mix.

As I watched José swim away, I had a sense that things might not go well for him so I decided to swim after him. The current was strong that day and the waves were high. José made it about seventy yards before there was trouble, big trouble. Thankfully, I was a strong swimmer and soon caught up with a floundering José.

"I can't make it man! Help me!"

I moved in to lend him a hand but he was thrashing around and every time I got close enough to help, he pulled me under.

I tried reasoning with him.

"José, relax and let me help," but in his state of panic he couldn't hear me.

Finally I did the only thing I could. I let him wear himself out to the point that he was so tired, he couldn't stay above water. I had to let him drown (at least it looked that way to him) to help him. When he was completely exhausted, I grabbed him and swam back to shore.

God did that for me. I was convinced that if I fought hard enough, knew enough, preached enough, studied enough, gave enough, loved enough or did enough, somehow the promises in the Bible would be made available to me. So I kept fighting the current, until I "swung myself out." But what I discovered from the Bible was God's grace doesn't require me to do anything. That's what makes grace, grace. This book isn't for everyone. If you are where you want to be in your relationship with God, put this book aside. Or, maybe you are in the midst of a trial, convinced your actions alone will somehow change the outcome of whatever you are facing. If so put down this book. But for those who are "weak and heavy laden" from carrying the burden you thought was yours to carry, and are finding your walk with God too much to handle, read on.

It is my sincere hope and desire that when you see grace in the Light of His Word you will experience the grace that changes everything!

Chapter 1

The Power of Grace

And he said unto me, My grace is sufficient for thee: for my strength is made perfect in weakness. Most gladly therefore will I rather glory in my infirmities, that the power of Christ may rest upon me. 2 Corinthians 12:9 KJV

Grace has the potential to right every wrong, calm every storm, and restore every relationship. Unfortunately this grace lies dormant in the lives of many who both need and want this grace, often from a lack of knowledge. The prophet Hosea made this simple yet profound statement as he was prompted by God;

My people are destroyed for lack of knowledge: ....Hosea 4:6 KJV

Why is this word so powerful? In the kingdom of God, His words hold power. *When God makes His people a promise, hell trembles.* Sadly, many people never fully understand God's grace the way God wants His people to understand it. Instead, life has a way of defining things for us, based on our own personal experience. From a human standpoint, grace isn't something we regularly experience. Lawsuits choke our courts. Stories of injustices from victims abound on the evening news. Experiences from our past tell us that grace doesn't exist in the way the Bible describes grace, so we settle.

What if we were left to define grace by what we have experienced? How would we explain grace to a visitor from another planet? What is our understanding of grace as believers? If we do not understand the real meaning of grace, we can never experience the true power of grace.

In the Garden of Eden, Adam and Eve were in a state of perfect togetherness with God. Imagine walking with God, admiring all he had created, and realizing that you were the only person on earth. He had created everything in front of your eyes, for you and you alone. There were no wars, no contentions, only perfect unity. From our experiences, it is difficult, if not impossible, to conceive of such a relationship in such a place. In our corporate worlds and in ministry, there are hills to climb, battles to win, wealth to acquire and reputations to make. But life for Adam and Eve was different. They lived by grace. All they had and all they would ever need was given to them by God. Adam and Eve were, for an unknown amount of time, completely content. God's grace was sufficient. But much like the humans of today it just wasn't enough.

In Genesis, we read a familiar story that is the foundation for all stories that would be written in the history of mankind: humanity's battle with humanity. We have, through the fall that happened that day, an inner restlessness that whispers, *more, more.* Our fight, at first glance, seems to be a battle with many adversaries. However, in reality it is a battle with ourselves. True, the serpent was there in the garden, but it was Eve who physically picked the fruit. The serpent didn't shake the tree to dislodge the fruit. The serpent didn't take a bite to show how juicy the fruit was. Instead, he whispered to Eve. And that whisper sparked something within Eve. Was she missing something? Was God holding out on her? After all, Adam was around first, maybe God and Adam were in this together!

From Jewish tradition, creation happened in a way which left creation incomplete. In other words, for creation to be complete, we have to help. Our efforts help the Creator create! From other religious teachings we find mankind struggling to appease one of many gods who hold the fate of humanity in his or her hands. Some claim we are fallen gods mired here on earth until our time is complete and, having given enough effort, we may reacquire our godly status. All have a common denominator. Our efforts make things happen. *Grace is not opposed to our efforts, but to our earning God's favor through our efforts.*

No matter which faith or religious teaching a person has been introduced to, there is, at its core, humanity struggling against all odds to get to this higher power. Religion has often been explained as humanity's attempt to get to God.

But not the Gospel of Jesus Christ. It's the opposite; it is God's attempt to get to man. That's grace.

The power of grace lies in the initiator of that grace: God Himself and His infinite power.

I remember, as a child, reading through the Old Testament and thinking to myself how little room for error there was when it came to following God. Whole cities burned, people were wiped off the face of the earth by all manner of calamities, such as earthquakes, floods, snakes, lions, tigers and bears. I learned at an early age that God didn't play around when it came to doing the right thing! And pity the person who questioned that. Many Sunday mornings I heard about how God loved me and in the same breath that God had a spot reserved for me in hell if I messed up! So you can bet – I was told betting will get you to hell too! – I was going to do everything possible to ensure this was not going to happen to me. As a result, I would respond to the invitation the preacher gave at the end of service. I would leave my pew and walk the sinner's walk down the aisle to confess my sins from the previous week at the altar.

Looking back, I realize I had done everything I had been told to do in the Scriptures: believe, confess, and accept. But what escaped me was the idea that all of those concepts were embodied in two words: *total surrender.* I was comfortable with giving Jesus my bad

3

stuff, but my good stuff I could handle. He could take all the lying cheating, stealing, disrespectful attitude, anger, and laziness and the list of wrongdoings goes on. But all the good things like loyalty, love, honor, good work ethic and honesty I would keep for myself and use those good things for Him. It seemed like a good approach, and it's an approach that many take, but the results were disastrous.

Anything not given to God will be at odds with God.

In the church I serve, we have a team of pastors who work well together. In fact, we really like each other. That may seem odd because, after all, isn't this the way church leadership should work? But I know from experience that even on boards that appear to have it all together, there are problems that no one in the church (except for the leaders) knows about. Thankfully, this is not the case with the team I am blessed to serve alongside. In fact, because of our close relationship, we are excited to learn from one another. A key element of spiritual growth is the willingness to learn what God is teaching us through others we are blessed to have in our lives. Often the person whom God uses doesn't even realize this is happening!

Dan, our Pastoral Care Pastor, was retiring from his position as a university music professor and orchestra maestro. In celebration of his retirement, he and his wife, Pam, were planning to have a retirement party at their house. To prepare, he needed a truck and asked if he could borrow mine to move some chairs and tables. Since I had planned a short trip the same day he needed my truck, we decided to trade vehicles.

We met at church and I began to explain the things he needed to know about my truck.

"Sometimes, when you try to start the truck, you have to grab the gear shift and put pressure on the handle to move the key in the ignition. When it rains, you'll need to put the fuse in the fuse panel for the wipers. I had to pull the fuse because the switch broke and the wipers wouldn't turn off. You just have to make sure they are in the right position when you pull the fuse or they will be in the way when you are driving. The driver's door doesn't shut all the way, so you might get wet if it rains. But rest assured it won't come open when you are driving. When you first start the truck, there is a banging from beneath the dash, but that goes away after about 15 seconds. When you shut off the truck, it'll make the same noise for another 15 seconds or so. Don't rub up against the sides of the truck when you are moving your things or the rust may cut you. And one last thing: I don't recommend you park this thing in your driveway because it leaks oil."

As I was explaining the "nuances" of my "sweet ride," Dan and Pam were in tears laughing. Looking back, I actually think I saw a glimmer of fear in their eyes. When I finished telling them all they would need to know about my truck and gave them my keys, they handed over the keys to their "sweet ride", a pristine, garaged, mint-condition Thunderbird coupe! I got the better end of this deal! In that moment, God's grace was shown to me in such an applicable way that I included what happened that morning in my sermon for that following weekend and in this book.

No doubt, my truck has issues, but it does have its redeeming qualities. It always starts (even though it smokes at first); it is a truck and will haul what I need to haul. These redeeming qualities made my truck useful to Dan.

That's often how we view our lives in the Kingdom of God. The "bad stuff" we willingly give to God. But our good attributes, the things we like about ourselves we hold onto. Again, *anything not given to God will be at odds with God.*

These good traits are what we often rely upon to find our worth. The power of God's grace finds strength in our weakness. The Apostle Paul, whom we'll discuss further in this chapter, understood this spiritual truth.

> And he said unto me, My grace is sufficient for thee: for my strength is made perfect in weakness. Most gladly therefore will I rather glory in my infirmities, that the power of Christ may rest upon me. 2 Corinthians 12:9 KJV

The more good we find in ourselves, the more likely we will continue to try living by our own strength. When I handed over my truck keys to Dan, I gave him the entire truck. When we give our lives to Jesus Christ He wants our whole life.

The only downside of my story is I had to give the car back! God's grace is forever.

DAVID

Reading through the Old Testament in search of grace can be a daunting task. Wars and battles, family splits and brotherly quarrels abound. But in the story of David we find a true example of grace.

King David, as he would later be known, was the youngest of eight sons. Much of his young life was spent tending sheep in the fields, protecting his flock from wild animals that roamed the countryside. From the vague description we have of David, we find that he wasn't the biggest of the brothers nor was he specially gifted in any way that would set him apart. In fact, being the eighth brother granted David the unenviable position within his family as the "remnant." The number seven in Hebrew culture was the number of completion; the number eight was considered the left over or remnant. So while his brothers were preparing for battle with their Philistine enemy, David was tending the sheep far from the din of battle.

We first read of David's courage when he steps out onto the field of battle against the Philistine champion, Goliath. Armed with a shepherd's sling and five smooth stones, David stepped on the battlefield to defend the honor not of his people, but his God. With an aim honed by countless nights of defending his flock in the wild, David toppled the nine foot giant with a well-placed rock to the forehead. King Saul declared David a national hero and gave David command of a great army as a reward. But King Saul overstepped his bounds as king.

Kings ruled the kingdom. Priests were the go-between for God and His people. These roles were distinctly separate. King Saul grew impatient while waiting for the prophet Samuel to arrive and preside over the sacrifice in the city of Gigal. King Saul assumed the role of a priest and performed the sacrifice himself. This act cost Saul his kingdom. God intervened, secretly appointing David the new king of Israel by the hand of the prophet Samuel.

David kept this secret and served Saul until Saul, overcome with jealousy because of David's prowess in battle and his numerous accolades put a price on David's head. But David loved King Saul and would not take what was rightly his without a direct command from God, so he ran. David ran for eight years, with Saul constantly chasing him. Saul's sole purpose in life became killing David.

David had his chances to take what was rightfully his many times. Once, King Saul took a break from chasing David in the exact same cave that David had chosen to hide. While King Saul was distracted, David crept close to Saul and cut the hem of Saul's garment to show how close he had been, but he wouldn't take the life of Saul. David showed Saul grace, even though he could have retaliated for how Saul treated him. David even crept into Saul's camp one night and took Saul's spear and water bottle. But he refused to take Saul's life. Eventually, David grew tired of dodging Saul and settled in the land of his old enemy, the Philistines.

The Philistines, once again, assembled for war against the Israelites. Tragically, during a battle with the Philistine enemy, King Saul, along with all his sons, was killed. David assumed the throne of Israel as King with great sorrow and a heavy heart. In 1 Samuel, we can read about the many acts of grace found in the story of King David. However, it was what occurred after David ascended the throne that truly shows us the power of grace.

After David became king, he began to better organize his kingdom. David and his army fought and won many battles. As the dust of battles settled, David's thoughts returned to his friend Jonathan, King Saul's son.

Jonathan had been a dear friend to David, even when Saul had sworn to kill him. In fact, so deep was their friendship that Jonathan tried to protect David from his father's wrath, going as far as to reason with Saul about David. It's not often in life we have those true friends who, even in the face of personal danger, stand with us. Jonathan was this sort of friend. They were so close that they were more like brothers than friends.

David, remembering his close relationship with Jonathan and, no doubt, still grieving over the loss of his friend, asked his servant if there were any of Jonathan's family still alive. His servant, Ziba, told him of a son that resided in a place called Lodebar. His name was Mephibosheth. In Hebrew, Mephibosheth means "to dispel shame." Lodebar means "place of no pasture."

Many of the people in those days tended sheep and other grazing stock. Much like today, good land was a precious commodity. Shepherds looked for places of good pasture to feed their flocks of sheep or other animals. Since there very few people who would reside or even visit such a place as Lodebar, it must have seemed like the perfect hiding place. Mephibosheth, "dispeller of shame," was hidden in a place where no one would ever find him, a "place of no pasture." No one cared about a place where no one wanted to go.

During the times when kings ruled, when a king assumed a throne, efforts were made to ensure any future rival to the throne would be dispatched – usually assassinated – to secure the place of the current monarch. Mephibosheth hid himself where no one would stumble upon him and report his whereabouts to the new king. But somehow, Ziba knew where he was hiding. Perhaps it was because of Mephibosheth's physical deformity.

After his grandfather and father were killed in battle, Mephibosheth's nurse, in her haste to secure the young prince's safety, accidentally dropped him, causing serious damage to his feet. It was a condition the Bible refers to as "lame." The Hebrew word for lame means someone who "hops." Whatever the physical deformity was, it was serious enough to warrant him living in the house of another.

It is possible Mephibosheth wasn't able to take care of himself. Upon hearing about Mephiboseth, David sent his servant to retrieve him. Imagine how Mephibosheth must have received the news of David's invitation. "He's found me and I can't get away because of these feet, these twisted, useless feet. How can I leave and find a new hiding place? Someone had to carry me here!"

Resigned to whatever fate awaited him, Mephibosheth entered the king's house. As soon as Mephibosheth saw King David, he fell at the feet of David. But this story has a happy ending.

When David saw Mephibosheth, he not only invited him to eat at his table, but he restored all the land that had been his grandfather's. He even made the palace Mephibosheth's permanent residence. Grace changed everything. Such is God's grace to us.

Because of grace, we have access to the King. Mephibesheth's story tells us about the access we have to God because of the sacrifice made by Jesus Christ. In the Old Testament, the priest went into the temple once a year behind the sacred curtain into the holy of holies. The priest, during those days, was the only person allowed to go before God. But even with this permission came certain conditions. To enter the temple not properly clothed and prepared meant certain death. The priests had to clean themselves up. Ceremonial washings and cleansings were required before any priest could enter this most holy of places.

Unfortunately, this Old Testament standard is often revisited in our New Testament churches. How many times have we heard it said that Jesus wants us to come to Him just as we are? Then, after we make that connection with Him, we are informed by some well-meaning saint that now we have to clean up our act? Grace is exactly the opposite.

Just like Mephibosheth, who couldn't make himself "unlame," we can't make ourselves any better. Think of how ridiculous it would have been if David would have said to Mephibosheth, "Now that you're here, in order to stay, do something about those feet!"

God's invitation of grace is available to anyone who wants it. God's grace doesn't ever rely on what we can do before or after Christ. Grace relies on the finished work of Jesus. David invited Mephibosheth to live and eat in his palace. Mephibosheth changed his place of residence. Mephosheth had a new identity. He was no longer called Mephibosheth, the lame grandson of Saul. He was now called Mephibosheth, friend of the king. Mephibosheth could come and go within the palace whenever he wanted, based only on the invitation of David.

Mephibosheth was never denied access to the king. There were no guards escorting him away from the king because he didn't belong. He was there by invitation of the King. He had free run of the entire kingdom. Think of our place in the Kingdom. Because of the finished work of Christ, we have total access to God, period.

> For I am persuaded, that neither death, nor life, nor angels, nor principalities, nor powers, nor things present, nor things to come, nor height, nor depth, nor any other creature, shall be able to separate us from the love of God, which is in Christ Jesus our Lord. Romans 8:38–39 KJV

Now think for a moment about what resources were available to Mephibosheth because of his relationship with the king. His food, shelter and protection were all granted to him by the King. The only requirement placed on Mephibosheth was to live like a friend of the King. How many battles or heroic deeds do you think King David asked Mephibosheth to perform? None; he was lame! The only power Mephibosheth had was the power granted him by the king.

Mephibosheth never had to prove his worthiness to David; in fact it was just the opposite. His helpless state put him in the perfect position to receive grace from David. Grace changes everything!

SAUL

> And Saul, yet breathing out threatenings and slaughter against the disciples of the Lord, went unto the high priest, And desired of him letters to Damascus to the synagogues, that if he found any of this way, whether they were men or women, he might bring them bound unto Jerusalem. Acts 9:1-2 KJV

Born a Roman citizen, from the Israelite tribe of Benjamin, a Pharisee of Pharisees, Saul of Taurus was not a person to tangle with. His knowledge of the Torah (law) was unparalleled in the synagogues. He had heard of this new religion that had begun to grow in Jerusalem and the surrounding areas. Saul was going to do all he could to ensure those who chose this path, "the way," as it was called, would pay dearly for their decision. It wasn't that long ago he held the coats of those who stoned one of these heretics to death. Saul was on his way to Damascus to obtain letters of permission from the high priests there to search for these "followers of the way." Once these heretics were found they would be brought back in chains to Jerusalem. There they were to stand trial for their treasonous actions against God.

As he neared his destination, a bright light and a loud voice from heaven changed his plans. Saul was met by the risen Christ. This encounter left him blind and helpless. The men who were under his command were forced to lead him stumbling blindly into Damascus and leave him there by himself. For three days, Saul couldn't see. For three days, he went without food or water. For three days, he was alone with his thoughts, processing what had taken place.

On the other side of town, Ananias, a disciple of Christ, was having a disturbing conversation with the same risen Jesus that stopped Saul in his tracks on the way to Damascus.

> And there was a certain disciple at Damascus, named Ananias; and to him said the Lord in a vision, Ananias. And he said, Behold, I am here, Lord. And the Lord said unto him, Arise, and go into the street which is called Straight, and enquire in the house of Judas for one called Saul, of Tarsus: Acts 9: 10-11KJV

As we read these words written by Luke in the book of Acts, it would be easy to miss the gravity and potential repercussions of what might occur during this meeting with Saul. Ananias didn't.

> Then Ananias answered, Lord, I have heard by many of this man, how much evil he hath done to thy saints at Jerusalem: And here he hath authority from the chief priests to bind all that call on thy name. Acts 9: 13-14 KJV

"What if Saul has papers with my name on them? What if Saul is looking for me?" These are questions that might have been on the mind of Ananias when Jesus directed his mission.

Saul was there when Stephen was stoned; that was a well-known fact. The stoning that had occurred that day had shown the followers of "the way," how far the Jewish high priests would go to stop this new religion.

Put yourself in the sandals of Ananias. What would your response be? I have asked myself the same question. Would I go to Saul? Without a touch of grace from God, this might have been another "Jonah" story. Run the other way!

Ananias' name in the Hebrew means "The Lord has favored." From the grace Ananias received, he gave. The man whose name meant favored, shared the favor he received from Jesus with a man who was to become the loudest orator of God's grace the Kingdom had ever seen. Grace would change everything for everyone who would come into contact not only with Saul, but with the resurrection power given to him by Jesus.

Saul had been touched by God's grace and his life had changed, just like his name. He was no longer known as Saul of Tarsus to those he met, but Paul, servant of Jesus Christ, sharing the grace he had received from Jesus with anyone who would listen. In Paul's thirteen letters to the various churches he started and to the people he met during his travels, grace reigns supreme. Paul uses the word grace a total of ninety-one times and always includes it in his salutation at the beginning of each letter.

The laws he lived by and taught were fulfilled by grace. All the New Testament authors were touched by this same grace. Their letters to other believers resoundingly echoed with the finality of God's grace, and how short they fell in God's eyes by their own actions apart from His grace.

> For the law having a shadow of good things to come, and not the very image of the things, can never with those sacrifices which they offered year by year continually make the comers thereunto perfect. Hebrews 10:1 KJV

What the law was unable to do, Jesus completed. The law, until that time, had directed Paul's steps and provided him the confidence to act, but not the holiness grace promised. The grace of God in Jesus Christ compelled him to share a message that changed everything for everyone forever.

Chapter 2

Grace Defined

> The LORD did not set his love upon you, nor choose you, because ye were more in number than any people; for ye were the fewest of all people. Deuteronomy 7:7 KJV

What is grace? To fully understand the power of grace, we must understand what grace is. Our understanding of grace should be formed by how the Bible defines grace. The Bible records accounts of real people with real life problems. The people of the Bible often expected God to hear and answer their petitions, even when they deserved the exact opposite.

The writers of the Old Testament were Jewish, or, more correctly stated, Hebrews. The word Hebrew means "to cross over." Abraham, the father of the Jewish nation, commanded by God, left his homeland in Ur (somewhere in Babylon), with his family in tow, to travel to a distant land on the other side of the river Euphrates. Hence the name Hebrew, because he *crossed over the river*. From Abraham and his family God built a nation of people, the Jewish nation.

Looking back at the history of the Jewish nation, God actively protects and provides for this small nation of people. Battles were fought and won; entire segments of land were given by God to these people. They were known throughout the region as a nation blessed by God. From humble beginnings, this nation was handpicked by God because.....well, according to God, there was no reason at all.

> The LORD did not set his love upon you, nor choose you, because ye were more in number than any people; for ye were the fewest of all people. Deuteronomy 7:7 KJV

God never gives them a reason for His choice of people. He simply chooses them. No merit set them apart, no great men of God that would "sweeten the deal" for God. But this nation was chosen to herald the promise of the coming Messiah. The prophets of this nation foretold the coming of this Messiah (anointed One) and the people waited eagerly for this promised King. This Messiah King would right the wrongs and bring peace to the earth.

Grace is defined as "unmerited mercy." Biblically grace is defined as "unmerited divine favor," meaning nothing can be done to earn this favor. Long before God chose these particular people to build a nation, God showed His grace to another man, Noah.

IN THE EYE OF GRACE

The first mention of the word grace we find in the Bible is in the account of Noah. Noah and his family were the tenth generation after creation. During those ten generations of human existence on earth, according to Genesis 6, humanity's wickedness was only getting worse. Violence was everywhere. Life had become a cheap commodity. People had not only turned their backs on God, they had turned their backs on one another. From God's vantage point, it was time to step in and wipe out everything.

> And the LORD said, I will destroy man whom I
> have created from the face of the earth; both man,
> and beast, and the creeping thing, and the fowls of
> the air; for it repenteth me that I have made them.
> Genesis 6:7 KJV

> Amid all the chaos and wickedness, Noah caught
> God's eye. But Noah found grace in the eyes of the
> LORD. Genesis 6:8 KJV

When Noah found grace in the eyes of God, his future changed. God's grace assured Noah he would not share the same fate as the rest of humanity. God told Noah that He was going to send a worldwide flood to wipe out the people and animals of the earth. For a moment, put yourself in Noah's sandals. Imagine God reveals to you that you and your family would be the only human survivors during this flood. What would be your reaction? Relief at first, then sorrow? Anger?

Many people question the love of God towards humanity because of the devastating flood during the time of Noah. The question often asked is, "How could a loving God wipe out an entire population of people and animals?" But we have only to look at the first two brothers, Cain and Able, to see that man was already doing a good job of killing himself.

In other biblical accounts of God wiping out entire cities, we read how the recipient of the bad news would argue with God. Abraham argued with God when God told him that He was going to destroy Sodom and Gomorrah. Further on in Genesis, Jacob wrestled with God. The prophet Jonah actually ignored God's direction and ran. Not so with Noah. Noah didn't ask why. Noah didn't question God. Instead, he set about building an ark. It seems Noah agreed with God. Could things have really been that bad?

Bad news bombards us constantly in our world today. We expect bad news when we turn on our television sets. This may sound like a generalization, but it's true. Try this little test over the next week.

Record the number of bad news stories during the evening's news hour broadcast and note how many good news stories there are during the same broadcast. If you don't have a week, just try this exercise for a night. Society is used to bad news. Those stories may appall us, but do they surprise us?

Now imagine living in a society where people live for six or eight hundred years. There was no media to broadcast the evil actions of humanity. Stories of interest were told and retold over hundreds of years. And sometimes the news stories you heard were about one of your own family members either committing a crime or becoming the victim of one of these crimes. What if the bad news stories we heard on the television, more often than not, contained names of family members or people we personally knew? What would our opinion of humanity be if we knew many of the people the "news stories" were about? It is a different proposition when news stories affect us personally.

Shortly after the attacks on the World Trade Center, I met a woman who lost a loved one during that attack. Her loss wasn't just a story she watched unfold on the television; it was personal.

In the midst of all the bad news of the day, Noah received even more bad news. A flood was coming. But this news may have been more confusing than frightening for Noah. Up until the day the rain started, it had never rained on earth. The Bible tells us there was a mist that watered the ground. God gave Noah a message of grace because Noah found favor in God's eyes. Noah received the news by faith; he had never experienced rain, but he put his trust in God. God told Noah to build a boat, a really big boat! If there were boats around at that time, this boat Noah was building was unlike any boat anyone had ever seen.

From the story of Noah and the first mention of grace in the Bible, we see how when God extends His grace to a person things change. We are not sure of how Noah's life looked before the flood, other than we are told he "tilled the ground." Noah went from a farmer to master boat builder, all because of grace he found with God.

17

Grace, for many, means a get out of trouble free card. If things don't change in the life of those who have received grace, then possibly what they received wasn't grace. Maybe they were extended a courtesy that allowed them to temporarily rise above their immediate situation, but with no lasting effects. Grace leaves a mark. Grace motivates us to fall in step with God. God had a plan and He invited Noah to be a part.

From birth, God chose Noah to be a part of His plan. Noah's name in the Hebrew means "rest." While Noah's life may not have been one of rest and relaxation, God's plan meant that, through Noah, humanity would have rest from the evil that plagued the earth. This plan of God's grace was bigger. Much like trying to envision the ark Noah built, it's hard to wrap our minds around God's big promise of grace to us!

Consider the enormity of this task God gave Noah. The ark was a three-story boat 450 feet long and 75 feet wide. Noah was a farmer, not a carpenter. Without a clear message from God, he would never have completed the task. It took Noah around 70 years (biblical scholars differ on this point) to complete the ark. During those years, Noah worked every day except Saturdays. If we do the math and consider days off for the Sabbath rest, Noah could have labored almost 21,000 days to complete the ark and gather the animals. But to fully understand grace, it's important to remember that Noah found grace before the he undertook this task. Beginning a mission without God's grace empowering that task is a recipe for disaster.

It is likely God will not call upon us to build an ark. But as His people, we are called to many different areas of ministry in His Kingdom. To even attempt a task without first understanding we have found grace and acceptance in the eyes of God, apart from our actions, will lead to burnout and frustration. Just like Noah, *we work from God's grace, not for His grace.* Jesus Christ accomplished God's promise of grace to us. Our efforts don't add to His grace. In other words, we don't work to please God.

After Noah's account in the Bible, the story of God's grace gathers speed and power. God chose a people who, by His own admission, had no redeeming qualities. From this choice emerged the Jewish nation. From this Jewish nation would come the Deliverer, the Anointed One, the Christ. But between God's graceful choice and the cross on Golgotha, there would be a battle that raged between God and His sworn enemy Satan.

To fully comprehend grace and its effect in our lives, we should examine how this newly formed nation viewed God's Grace.

In the Jewish language, grace comes from a root word meaning to "stoop or bend down in kindness to an inferior." All through the pages of the Old Testament we read about how God, from His place of perfection, "stooped" to extend kindness and mercy to the Jewish nation. But we also read of how when they refused this grace, God let them have their own way.

When God lets people have their way, bad things happen. Often in our attempt to justify our actions, we often place the blame for bad things on God, when, in reality, God is allowing us to receive what we wanted.

From this Old Testament model comes much of what we know about God's grace, which, for many of us, meant do things this way or you will pay the price! However, we must remember God was preparing the way for a Savior. This savior would come through the Jewish tribe of Judah. Much of what took place in the Bible was because God was safeguarding His plan for this coming Savior. Just having the choice to decide to do wrong means God's grace is still at work in our own disobedience.

God's Gifts Of Grace

Growing up during the 70's in the South meant that in some shape, form, or fashion, a person heard about God. Praying before meals or a stock-car race was always more of a tradition than a spiritual act, until I began to explore my faith. My faith was handed down and accepted without question. My beliefs were adopted from those who knew more than me, and I trusted those people to tell me what I needed to know about God. It wasn't until I began to examine my beliefs, in light of what the Bible said, that I became increasingly aware that I didn't have the whole story.

Much of what we know in our spiritual lives reflects the culture or beliefs of our surroundings. I'm not a big fan of defining a person's beliefs by using terms such as liberal or conservative; this only serves to widen the gap we already experience in our churches today. But these are terms which many are unfortunately familiar with and serve the purpose of explaining a point.

Whether we are from a more liberal culture or very conservative background, chances are that our spiritual life will reflect this. Understand, I'm not stating being conservative or liberal is wrong, *but if we are more conservative or liberal than Scripture dictates, our opinion becomes Scripture.*

A conservative hot topic during my childhood was the topic of charismatic churches. According to my trusted sources, these charismatic churches were all about emotions and feeling good and were often accused of watering down the gospel. Because of those warnings, I never stepped foot in *those* churches.

The term charismatic comes from the Greek word *charisma*, which means gift, and is always used in the Bible as representing a divine endowment. The Greek word grace, finds its root in the word for gift. That word is *charis.* The Bible teaches that any church which claims Jesus as the head of that church should be a "charismatic" church, because from God's grace comes these gifts given to His people to carry out the mission of God on earth. A charismatic church is simply a church that accepts and employs these spiritual gifts for His purposes, glory and honor.

In fairness, there has been gift abuse in these "charismatic" churches. This abuse gives other churches that embrace these God-given gifts and use them properly a bad name and the moniker of "one of *those* churches." However, another form of abuse is neglect.

Those churches who deny the gifts of the Spirit, from a scriptural standpoint, stand in direct contradiction to what the Bible says is available to all believers.

> And He gave some as apostles, and some as prophets, and some as evangelists, and some as pastors and teachers, for the equipping of the saints for the work of service, to the building up of the body of Christ; *until we all attain to the unity of the faith,* and of the knowledge of the Son of God, to a mature man, to the measure of the stature which belongs to the fullness of Christ. Ephesians 4:11-13 (italics mine)

God's grace leaves a mark! When grace is fully realized, there will be a physical manifestation. Much like Noah when he found grace in the eyes of God and built an ark, when we receive this same grace, what has happened on the inside will show itself on the outside. God changes the heart and, from that change, physical actions result. The answer is not trying harder, but receiving what we have been promised.

THE GIFT OF TONGUES

> And they were all filled with the Holy Ghost, and began to speak with other tongues, as the Spirit gave them utterance. Acts 2:4 KJV

> And when Paul had laid his hands upon them, the Holy Ghost came on them; and they spake with tongues, and prophesied. Acts 19:6 KJV

In the New Testament, the Bible often speaks of tongues, which are a physical manifestation of God's Spirit communing and reaching out to His children. Sometimes these gifts are abused, but we shouldn't base our understanding of how God moves on misrepresentation of His glory in others.

As a new pastor, I began meeting for a time of prayer with a pastor of one of *those* churches. I'll have to admit that, because of bad teaching in my youth, I was on guard when we first started meeting. I really didn't know what to expect. To my surprise and elation, those times of prayer built me up, encouraged me in my role as a pastor and strengthened me as a believer. This pastor was keenly aware of his surroundings and understood how many people viewed the gift of tongues. He never spoke or prayed in tongues during our time of prayer, but we talked about this gift at length many times during our time together.

As our relationship grew, I had the opportunity to speak at his church on one Sunday evening. I didn't really know what to expect. After the service, we gathered in small groups and began to pray. One of the ladies in our group began speaking in tongues. I admit, I was a little uncomfortable, but I was on a journey to get everything that God had planned for me. Soon another person began speaking in tongues in my circle. But these new "speakers" weren't making me nervous, in fact, I was comfortable and it didn't raise any red flags. But I began to see why this practice repels people who don't believe in tongues or think that it's not a gift for today's church. It's out of the realm of a "normal" Christian experience. Many times, when the unfamiliar confronts us, we are unsure of how to know what is real and what is not. But God doesn't leave us in the dark on this topic.

From Scripture we are told the purpose of these gifts:

> And He gave some as apostles, and some as prophets, and some as evangelists, and some as pastors and teachers, *for the equipping of the saints for the work of service,* to the building up of the body of Christ; *until we all attain to the unity of the faith,* and of the knowledge of the Son of God, to a mature man,

to the measure of the stature which belongs to the fullness of Christ. Ephesians 4:11-13 (italics mine)

Now there are varieties of gifts, but the same Spirit. And there are varieties of ministries, and the same Lord. There are varieties of effects, but the same God who works all things in all persons. But to each one is given the manifestation of the Spirit *for the common good.* 1 Corinthians 12:4-7 (italics mine)

Of all the gifts, the gift of tongues seems to be a point of contention among many believers. Many believe the gifts have ceased while others believe the Bible clearly states the gifts are still in operation within the church. From Scripture we see the divine purpose of these gifts: to build God's earthly church. The best way to "test the spirits," as John tells us to do in the Bible, is to see if the person or persons which are employing their gifts, any gifts, is bringing attention to God or to themselves.

I don't have the gift of tongues; however, I see from Scripture that Paul uses the present tense when talking about these gifts. He writes "to each one is given." It amazes me how many times I missed the fact that the gifts are referred to in the present tense. The promises of deliverance and forgiveness are referred to in the past tense. This would mean, *we are denying the present help sent from God, as well as the past work Jesus accomplished on the cross.*

Many times, God moves people to speak like this and, if we are in the same Spirit, we'll know what is true and from God. Rather than letting our experiences dictate what is true, we should examine what the Bible has to say about these things. What we may find is that our definition of a "normal Christian experience" may need to be re-examined.

Speaking in tongues, whether in a heavenly language as some say, or a foreign language, is another form and manifestation of grace in a believer's life. God doesn't want His children ignorant of the blessings

23

we already have, such as deliverance or forgiveness, or those waiting to be revealed, such as spiritual gifts. God's Spirit tells us what is real and what is not. Often, from experience, we try to reason from the flesh things that are spiritual. But God gives His people the spiritual ability to reason these things of the Spirit.

> Now we have received, not the spirit of the world, but the Spirit who is from God, so that we may know the things freely given to us by God, which things we also speak, not in words taught by human wisdom, but in those taught by the Spirit, combining spiritual thoughts with spiritual words. But a natural man does not accept the things of the Spirit of God, for they are foolishness to him; and he cannot understand them, because they are spiritually appraised. 1 Corinthians 2:12-14

In the moment when God's Spirit and ours connect, God gives us an affirmation. We are in harmony with the Creator of the universe but, often because of our lack of attention toward Him and His purpose, we falter and get distracted. Sometimes, God's plans conflict with ours. I wonder what Noah had planned during those years he was building that ark? Whatever those plans were, he laid them down.

For the longest time, I tried to do all the "right" things to access the presence of God. It worked for a short time and with limited success. When I began to approach things of this world from the spiritual vantage point, things changed radically for me. This all had to do with grace.

We live our lives in a pressure cooker: deadlines, meetings, financial shortfalls, relationship problems, just to name a few obstacles. All these things have to do with living in this world among flesh and bone people. These same people can be the cause of these problems, so we need a higher solution. In short, if we caused these problems, it's a pretty sure bet we can't fix these problems. That's when God extends His grace from a place above all the problems. Our solutions to this life will never be found from this life. Instead, these solutions have to come from somewhere elsewhere the flesh can't go: The Spiritual. The heavenly place of God.

Paul wrote these words to the people at Ephesus: "By grace are you saved; through faith, not of ourselves, it is the gift of God." If you have spent any time in church, hopefully these words are familiar. But maybe these words have become too familiar. To fully understand how we are saved, we need to know what we were saved from. Understanding the meaning of salvation can show us how grace can change everything.

Chapter 3

Saved by Grace

> And the scripture, foreseeing that God would justify
> the heathen through faith, preached before the gospel
> unto Abraham, saying, In thee shall all nations be
> blessed. Galatians 3:8 KJV

The Gospel in its entirety tells the story of God's plan for humanity. It is a message of hope. Many times we receive the shortened version of the Gospel message: "Get saved or go to hell!" This message is one of condemnation instead of conviction, that a person is living in such a way that God has reserved a special place in hell just for them. But the reality is, *we don't have to do anything to go to hell; it's already our destination apart from Christ.*

It's no wonder many churches have become ineffective. *We hold people to standards of performance, rather than share the reality of our situation.* Without Christ we are doomed, even if we live a stellar life. Our situation is a result of who we are, not what we have done. Without a full revelation of this scriptural truth we will continue to wear ourselves out performing for grace!!

Many new believers begin to read the Bible starting with the New Testament. That's a good place to start, but it still will never give us the entire gospel. To fully understand the entire gospel, we need to go back to when it was first preached. Most would think that was when Jesus and His band of disciples walked the earth. But it happened long ago. In fact, it happened before the New Testament was written. We get clues to this if we read the opening chapters of the book in the New Testament named Hebrews. Although this letter is contained in the New Testament, it references many things that took place in the Old Testament. Without a clear understanding of the Old Testament scripture, this New Testament letter would make little sense.

Just like its name implies, it was written to the Hebrews, God's chosen people. The authorship of this book has always been debated. Some believe Paul wrote it, while others say it was a compilation of more than one writer. Some attribute it to one of Paul's students. Due to lack of hard evidence, it is still unclear who penned this letter. Hebrews can be called "the book of better." As the writer(s) begin, we see how, no matter what came before Jesus, all these things or people, such as the angels or Moses, paled in comparison to the Son of God who has redeemed humanity. Then we come to a curious statement in the opening lines of Hebrews chapter four.

> Therefore, let us fear if, while a promise remains of entering His rest, any one of you may seem to have come short of it. For indeed we have had good news preached to us, just as they also; but the word they heard did not profit them, because it was not united by faith in those who heard. Hebrews 4:1-2

According to the writer of Hebrews the "good news" or gospel preached to those reading this letter weren't the first recipients. The message had gone out to the original children of Israel thousands of years before. That's right! When the Israelites crossed through the sea with Moses in the lead, they were already recipients of the gospel! This message was actually given many years before to Abraham. In fact, Paul tells the churches in the province of Galatia the same thing.

> And the scripture, foreseeing that God would justify
> the heathen through faith, preached before the gospel
> unto Abraham, saying, In thee shall all nations be
> blessed. Galatians 3:8 *KJV*

Just like today, many who heard the message didn't understand it in its entirety. God told Abraham that the nations would be blessed through him, more specifically through his *seed*. Now enters the confusion.

The Jewish nation, while chosen by God, weren't the recipients of that grace through any birthright. If they were, that would mean by special birth through the right parents, a child could be found righteous. But that's not grace. If being born into the right family made us righteous, then our actions would grant us access to the grace of God.

Think for a moment of how racism has taken root in our culture because of this same mindset. Many believe being born the correct color or in the right part of the world makes one better than others. Fortunately this is not how God views humanity, even if humanity holds to this belief.

Paul corrects this idea of grace by birth right to the Jewish people in the churches at Galatia:

> Now the promises were spoken to Abraham and to
> his seed. He does not say, "And to seeds," as referring
> to many, but rather to one, "And to your seed," that
> is, Christ. Galatians 3:16

Whenever the word seed occurs in the Bible, it refers to offspring or children. Paul tells us here the promise God made through Abraham wasn't for the whole nation but for one person: Jesus Christ. The world would be blessed through these people, not by these people. The Jewish nation was chosen to carry this message to the world and, through their lineage, The Savior would come. This Savior would save the world from their sins and put things right in their hearts. The "seed," Jesus Christ, would do what humanity would never be able to do. God communicated His message clearly, but it was distorted over time. Unfortunately, in many churches today, the gospel has been distorted in much the same way.

This good news was always God's plan. Even in the garden, when Adam and Eve ate the fruit, the plan was already in place. The gospel given to Abraham was for the Israelites not because they were uniquely qualified for God's salvation, but simply because God chose them to carry out His promised plan. The Jewish nation had taken the stance that, because of birthright, they were automatically saved, much like many people today who think their actions save them.

Notice that in this proclamation of the good news the absences of concepts like salvation or damnation to hell. Now, make no mistake, Jesus himself told us of a place that awaits anyone who rejects the message of God's news. But God calls us to Himself by promises of blessing, not threats of hell. Many people read the New Testament and adopt the teachings of Jesus when it comes to hell. We need to read deeper and understand the culture of that day. Jesus preached hell to the religious elite, the ones who thought they had the answer from God and held people in bondage to rules and regulations. We often forget this when we talk to people who have never read the Bible. They have no idea what is in the Bible, much less the gospel message.

FROM WHAT ARE WE SAVED BY GRACE?

Salvation may be even more misunderstood than grace. From my earliest memories, I heard, "get saved or you'll go to hell." That was the extent of my knowledge when it came to understanding salvation. It seemed the only thing I was saved from was hell. Understanding grace led me to a deeper understanding of salvation. I realized what I knew about salvation was acquired from others whose perception of grace was lacking. The result was an incomplete understanding of salvation. If asked, what would your explanation be of salvation? Can we really share the gospel in its entirety without clearly understanding salvation?

In Greek, the language in which the New Testament was written, the word salvation means much the same as it does in English; it means to be delivered. Some say that our salvation in Christ only covers our downward spiral into hell. But there is more, much more.

In both Hebrew and Greek, salvation means to be delivered not only from hell, but physical afflictions (anything that affects us in the natural) that we encounter. This also means our health, our finances and our relationships. The effects of living under these natural pressures often cause emotional problems, which are often at the root of many problems we face. Doctors tell us that many of our illnesses come from stress. Our salvation in Christ promises emotional healing.

The Bible tells us, "As a man thinks in his heart so he is." Much of what we face comes from misunderstanding our position in the Kingdom of God. We are no longer subjects or citizens of a kingdom full of disease and poverty. Instead, we have a Father who is rich in everything we need.

Step into any church, and you'll often find defeated and imprisoned believers. We hear a message of hope, but because of inconsistent and incomplete teachings, we don't receive the full message of salvation. We are often given the incomplete message that salvation only covers where I will spend eternity. This incomplete message short circuits the power of God. It's like we are sitting in a new car with a key that doesn't fit. The car looks good and smells new, but until we can actually start the car, we'll only stay in one place.

Many are in this predicament today. We have been given this gift of grace that looks great and sounds beautiful, but until we understand that this message is meant for us right now and not sometime in the future, we'll be stuck right where we are. In short, we are standing between God's promises and our complete salvation.

Now, understand that I'm in no way implying we can think things into existence. I cannot merely think of getting a new truck to replace my current truck and expect it to be so. But if I don't know that God has blessed me and empowered me to receive His blessings, I will always settle for second best in my life. I believe what God says about my situation, then the pressure is off to perform or not perform and it places my needs and concerns before the feet of God.

I may never get a new truck; I may have to walk or repair my old truck, but somehow God will move in this situation. I've seen this happen over and over again. I've had the opportunity to pray with and for many people. Sometimes these prayers were answered immediately. But there were times that my prayers weren't answered the way I wanted them answered. Sometimes God answered prayers in a way that I could have never have predicted. What I have discovered is that what many of us pray for is relief from the symptoms and not the cure. We ask God for help, but we hold tightly to things that continue to harm us. We are sitting in the new car, afraid to put the key in the ignition.

As I honestly evaluate my motivation in asking for something, sometimes I often find it to be self-centered. That's what I am referring to when I say complete salvation. God heals us and delivers us from the bad, evil motives that we have acquired in this life. Let's face it: life can be rough and we feel we have to take the "bull by the horns." It's our way of coping with bad things, to put up the walls and protect ourselves. But in the Kingdom of God, He is our protector. We can't serve God or see His power move on earth from behind emotional walls of protection. God doesn't demand those walls come down. He releases us to go past those walls. He gives us the freedom to live like we should, without fear.

Fear is a subtle enemy of any child of God. When we fear, this fear usually has to do with our own well-being. In the garden, when God confronted Adam about eaten fruit, do you remember Adam's response? He said Eve did it! In many situations, we feel the need to protect ourselves and pass the blame. The salvation God promises gives us the power to depend on Him in these sticky situations. It releases us from the deceptive fear that if we don't protect ourselves, no one else will.

For some, salvation means we are enduring our time here on earth until we get to heaven. Nothing here really matters because it's not our final destination. We are going through the motions of life and just trying to make it to heaven. God doesn't demand that we become passive citizens in the kingdom. In fact, He asks just the opposite. Paul addressed this apathetic approach in many of his letters to the New Testament churches.

> Be not overcome of evil, but overcome evil with good. Romans 12:21 KJV

God wants an active people who operate from a position of grace to change the flow of evil. God never tells us to just let things go and roll over. This "rolling over" often equates to what has become known as religious tolerance. In our culture, over the last few years, many have championed this need for religious tolerance.

I had the opportunity to speak on this topic at the church where I am on staff. As Sunday approached, I was nervous. The church has always been accused of intolerance. As a believer I often struggle with how to present the gospel message of hope, which is for everyone, without portraying a God who overlooks sin. But as I read through the pages of the Bible, I came to an understanding about religious tolerance.

Nowhere in the Bible does God tell us religious tolerance is an acceptable stand for any believer. In fact, what I came to understand was that religious tolerance undermines the grace given salvation God wants to extend through His Son. From an experience I had during the week prior to my speaking about this topic, I learned the danger of tolerance.

From years of manual labor, I am used to a certain amount of pain. Sad to say I haven't treated my body like a temple. From years of bending over repairing cars, my knees and back tend to bother me, especially during cold and cloudy days. But this pain is nothing compared to the pain of a toothache.

It began as a dull throb on Thursday and by Saturday morning the pain became unbearable. Unfortunately, since it was Saturday the dentist's office was closed. It was awful! I sat upright in our living room chair and didn't sleep for two nights before I could get into the dentist's office on Monday for some relief.

During that time, my wife called the dentist's emergency number to get some medication to relieve the pain I was in. I was prescribed some antibiotics and pain killers. Unfortunately for me, my tolerance for these types of pain medications is extremely high. I took the recommended dosage and nothing happened. I was still in excruciating pain. We contacted the dentist and were advised to double the dosage. The pain dulled but it never stopped.

Finally, on Monday, the dentist prescribed some stronger medication. When I arrived home, I had about three hours to wait before the oral surgeon could see me. I took the new stronger medication, along with all the other medications I had taken, combined to not only knock out the pain, but knock me out as well. When I awoke and began to get ready for my appointment, I felt queasy and progressively ill. On the way to the oral surgeon's office, the combination of medications I had taken made me sick.

Tolerance in the life of a believer is much like that experience I had with the pain killers. *The higher our tolerance to evil, the more likely we are to ingest those things into our lives.* Before we know it, what we were tolerating consumes us and the results are disastrous. It will poison us from the inside out. The state of our world is a glaring example of how tolerance can, in a very short time, contaminate everything. The world needs a message of hope only God's grace can provide. Salvation is the result of a person accepting God's grace. But letting things go and not standing up for right will never show the need for God.

Showing the grace of God doesn't mean we have to tolerate things that are clearly bad. This actually undermines the whole idea of God's grace. It lulls those who need God's grace into a false sense of security. Salvation by grace can only save when the recipient really wants it. There has to be a need. When we tolerate something evil, we may just be shutting the door of salvation in a person's face

The gospel's whole intent is to show us there is a better way. We can stand for what is right by living the gospel. Living the gospel will do what picket signs, church marquis and door to door evangelism will never do. Imagine the impact of simply walking across the street to help a neighbor rake their yard or just saying "hello" to someone we meet while out on a walk. If we don't live the gospel, this message of hope will be lost to the world. The gospel shows humanity the possibility of something better. Just because things have always been a certain way doesn't mean things have to remain the same.

COMPLETELY SAVED

We don't receive salvation by God's grace to just go to heaven. If salvation was only to get us into heaven, then we would have been taken to heaven the moment we received Jesus. Instead, there is a life to be lived here on earth. But remember this: this life we now live is by His grace alone; nothing we do or don't do will grant us any quicker access to peace. It is a "sounds too good to be true" proposition and understandably so. Nothing we have ever experienced can be compared to this salvation through faith.

Everything we have ever known comes with a contract or agreement that somehow holds sway over our lives. Usually what we receive isn't really a gift, but a wage, something we earn. From our parents, we received praise when we did good things. When we closed the deal at work, we were "the man." The things we received started with our actions. Salvation started with an action of God. We know that we can't save ourselves, but we often live by the motto, "pull ourselves up by our bootstraps." The Bible tells us, it is when we understand how totally helpless we are, we can be saved. After all, when was the last time you saw a person saved from drowning on dry land?

We need to be saved from ourselves. When life seems to go well, we have this sense that we are doing all the right things to get the right results. Mistakes mean failure, so the pressure to succeed can drive us crazy. We fear failure is right around the corner. Then from these failures, our emotional wounds can take us to a place where we think worse of ourselves than we should. This circle of bondage is what salvation through Jesus Christ brings to an end.

The salvation Jesus promises doesn't only save us from hell, but life as we know it. Salvation offers peace and rest that can only come from Jesus.

Trophies tarnish, money is spent, friends die, relationships crumble, but Jesus speaks these words into our lives: "I will never leave or forsake you." Jesus won't give up on us when we have given up on ourselves. Grace changes everything.

Chapter 4

Law and Grace

For sin shall not have dominion over you: for ye are not
under the law, but under grace. Romans 6:14 KJV

The Bible is divided into two distinct sections: The Old Testament
and the New Testament. Most people who have read the Bible
know the divisions, but often struggle with how to apply many of the
Old Testament laws and teachings. For those who have undertaken the
daunting task of reading the Bible from cover to cover, the Old and
New Testament almost seem at odds with one another. Stories abound
in the Old Testament of animal sacrifices and specific ordinances
for worship. The New Testament speaks of love and grace. But the
Old Testament tells us that, when properly understood, the stories
contained in it are somehow incomplete. From the prophets to the
kings, there is a longing for God's permanent presence in their lives.

Read the Psalms and notice the mountain top proclamations of
God's peace and presence, only to find a few lines further how this
same person feels lost and forgotten. This is the nature of The Old
Testament. For a short time, many heroes of the Old Testament rise
to prominence to complete a mission for God, only to stumble and
falter. The Old Testament shows us the need for a Savior who would
help us from the earliest of times. Consider the words of Job, which
most scholars agree is the oldest of the Old Testament writings.

"For He is not a man as I am that I may answer Him, That we may go to court together. "There is no umpire between us, Who may lay his hand upon us both. "Let Him remove His rod from me, And let not dread of Him terrify me. "Then I would speak and not fear Him; But I am not like that in myself. Job 9:32-35

Job, a man said to be righteous in the eyes of God, was desperate for a meditator. The Old Testament serves as a signpost that points to a coming Savior, Jesus Christ. The New Testament tells readers of a permanent solution: Jesus Christ. God's Son was the answer we needed, not laws and sacrifices that could not lead to permanent holiness in the eyes of God. We must look past the altar to something more permanent in order to fully grasp the Old Testament sacrifices and their meaning.

Many of us have things that have happened to us in our past life, before Christ, that show us the need for God's help in the present. For those who have come to this conclusion, the Bible and all those commandments should leave us with the knowledge that if we are relying on how good we are to get to God, we are in serious trouble. This was the conclusion Job came to when faced with the problem of pain and suffering.

But human nature is sold on the idea that if we make more rules, then things will get better. Turn on the news in the aftermath of a tragedy; you will notice the cry goes out for more rules and regulations. Historically, this hasn't worked in any country. No matter how many rules we institute, if those rules are not kept and enforced then the rules and laws mean nothing. Consider what the apostle Paul wrote to his protégé Timothy:

But we know that the Law is good, if one uses it lawfully, realizing the fact that law is not made for a righteous person, but for those who are lawless and

> rebellious, for the ungodly and sinners, for the unholy
> and profane, for those who kill their fathers or mothers,
> for murderers and immoral men and homosexuals and
> kidnappers and liars and perjurers, and whatever else is
> contrary to sound teaching, 1 Timothy 1:8-10

So if someone wants to break the law, more laws will not stop them.

THE LAW

Many people misunderstand the meaning and purpose of the laws in the Bible. When the laws are held to as a standard of excellence in the kingdom, grace will never be the end result. Instead, we wear ourselves out trying to live up to these laws rather than embracing the grace of God in Jesus. But there can be no grace unless there is a law that holds us accountable and ultimately shows us that we can't keep those laws of God without supernatural help.

To fully understand the laws found in the Old Testament requires a contextual study of those directives. To whom were these laws given and what purpose did they serve? What did the word "law" mean for the people of the Old Testament?

The Old Testament contains a historical account of the nation of Israel. Israel was given many blessings and through this nation the Savior of the world would be born. In the Hebrew language, the word "law" not only meant a precept or statute, but at its root the word actually meant "flow," similar to how a river flows to the ocean.

Whenever the nation of Israel would go in a direction contrary to God, there would be those men or women who would remind the nation to follow the law of God. These reminders weren't only to show the people how far out of touch they were with God, but to bring them back into the flow that God created to lead them to Him. The whole reason and intent of the law was to lead the people to a deeper understanding of God. But the law, while it was and is Holy, has its limitations: you and I. We were and are still unable to stay in God's flow without His help. His help is Jesus and His power is extended to all who claim Jesus as Savior.

In Jesus' time, this flow had been cut off. When He confronted the Pharisees, He addressed this serious breach of understanding and stood in direct contradiction to popular teaching the religious elite taught in the nation of Israel.

> But woe to you, scribes and Pharisees, hypocrites, because you shut off the kingdom of heaven from people; for you do not enter in yourselves, nor do you allow those who are entering to go in. Woe to you, scribes and Pharisees, hypocrites, because you devour widows' houses, and for a pretense you make long prayers; therefore you will receive greater condemnation. Woe to you, scribes and Pharisees, hypocrites, because you travel around on sea and land to make one proselyte; and when he becomes one, you make him twice as much a son of hell as yourselves. Matthew 23:13-15

Don't miss the implications of Jesus' words. The word "proselyte" means a person who had converted to Judaism. More specifically, they converted to the Pharisees' form of Judaism. But in their efforts to convert other people, the Pharisees began to make replicas of themselves.

The religious elite had actually placed "hedges" or barriers around the law of God to ensure they wouldn't break the law. From outside these "hedges," the law became a boundary not to cross. The standard of holiness was their ability to keep the law. *God's intent for the law was not to gauge our holiness, but to show us how short we fall in keeping His law.* Jesus says it would have been better if they had not converted at all.

It's not all that different today. Many claim allegiance to a denomination and adhere to that denomination's doctrine more tightly than they do the Gospel of Jesus Christ. Consider for a moment the sheer number of denominations in our world today. Depending on your sources, the number will be between 20,000 and 30,000 different denominations. Some sources place the number as high as 38,000. Does this sound anything like the words of Paul as he wrote about church unity?

> Endeavoring to keep the unity of the Spirit in the bond of peace There is one body, and one Spirit, even as ye are called in one hope of your calling; One Lord, one faith, one baptism, One God and Father of all, who is above all, and through all, and in you all. Ephesians 4:3-6 KJV

The Pharisees Sect began as a positive practice. After their exile and return to Jerusalem, the nation's leaders wanted to ensure they always remembered God so that what they had experienced would not happen again. But as time passed, they began to worship the laws instead of the lawgiver. Outside appearances began to take the place of inner purity. How people appeared on the outside began to take precedent over what God wanted to do on the inside.

> Woe to you, scribes and Pharisees, hypocrites! For you are like whitewashed tombs which on the outside appear beautiful, but inside they are full of dead men's bones and all uncleanness. So you, too, outwardly appear righteous to men, but inwardly you are full of hypocrisy and lawlessness. Matthew 23:27-28

Jesus was addressing the religious "keepers of the law" directly. If the laws' intent was to keep people holy, then the Pharisees would have been exempt from His warnings. The Pharisees were known for their strict adherence to the law. The Pharisees consisted of seven classes, all of which "specialized" in keeping these laws. One class of Pharisees, "the bruised Pharisee," was prone to running into walls while trying to avoid looking at a woman so as not lust after her.

But the things *we* do can and will only have an effect on the outside; what God does has an effect seen on the outside, but only because of an inward change. In the Hebrew the word law, means to "flow," it also means "to aim or point." In our culture, the word law means a boundary that we do not cross. The whole idea of law in our culture keeps lawlessness in check; the biblical idea of law brings to light in our spirit or "points" out to us the depravity of humanity. Paul knew this and wrote this to those believers in the Roman church:

> What shall we say then? Is the law sin? God forbid.
> Nay, I had not known sin, but by the law: for I had
> not known lust, except the law had said, Thou shalt
> not covet. Romans 7:7 KJV

The law itself is not bad, but like many in Paul's day, people today misunderstand its real purpose. Paul states the purpose of the law was to show us our true nature. Many people, both inside and outside the church, struggle with this idea. Those outside the church claim goodness based on a system that is reflective of biblical principles. But this system is still based on their goodness and how many of the laws they keep.

For example, some might state: "I'm a good person. I don't cheat on my wife; I don't beat my kids; I work and provide for my family. I don't steal." The list goes on. Unfortunately, in God's spiritual economy, these minimum standards aren't good enough.

Inside the church, believers struggle to keep the laws in order to please God, never realizing these laws had done what God had intended them to do: point them to God.

Even before Moses came down the mountain with the Ten Commandments, humanity had already lost its focus. God said,

41

"Listen to Me: don't eat the fruit of the tree of the knowledge of good and evil. Put no thing or person before Me." But Eve took a bite and then Adam did, and creation has struggled ever since. When God told the first humans not to eat of the forbidden fruit, it wasn't to set boundaries, but to show them God provided everything they would ever need.

In our society, the standard is much lower than in the Kingdom of God. Many of us break the laws of this world on a daily basis. We exceed speed limits. We lie on our taxes. We call in sick when we are well. If we get caught in those acts, there is usually a penalty to pay, even if we don't agree with the consequences. We can choose to ignore or break the laws in our world, but we can't choose the consequences of our actions when we stand before a judge. If the offense is bad enough, we will have a record. That's what law does! It keeps a record of offenses which can cost us certain freedoms or require a price to be paid for retribution. The only thing that can release us from these penalties is grace. Although grace is not something we encounter in our justice system, in God's Kingdom it's the basis of the gospel message of Jesus Christ.

The law keeps the outside; Grace changes the inside and forms the outside.

GRACE

God's laws were to show us the impossibility of changing human nature. If laws really changed us then eventually there would be no need for any law at all. To live under the law is to adhere to a set of guidelines. When Christ said, "It is finished," He set us free from the law to live in a way that the law always intended. The Bible tells us the laws were Holy, but we were not.

Many Christians still have difficulty with this freedom from the law. This freedom is not clearly understood, so it cannot be embraced. The freedom from the law ensures our freedom from sin.

> For sin shall not have dominion over you: for ye are not
> under the law, but under grace. Romans 6:14 KJV

> Wherefore the law is holy, and the commandment
> holy, and just, and good. Romans 7:12 KJV

Passages like the ones written above can cause confusion as we seek to understand God's intent for our lives. In one breath, Paul states we are free from the law and, therefore, free from sin. But further on he tells us the law is holy and good. Paul is telling us that we aren't under the penalty of the law, but the law still holds a place in our lives.

But understand this: *If we couldn't keep the laws before we met Jesus, what makes us think we can keep the law afterwards?*

For many, being a Christian is an act of will, and as long as we try to enforce our will, God can't move in our lives.

Grace has been defined as "undeserved favor or mercy." That's what makes grace so powerful and hard to conceptualize in our minds. We don't deserve it, yet God initiates this action and blessing towards us. Grace shows us the nature of God. The struggle we often face in our churches is the idea that grace has no strings attached.

But, if it did, it wouldn't be grace.

> For the wages of sin is death; but the gift of God is eternal
> life through Jesus Christ our Lord. Romans 6:23 KJV

From our experiences in the workplace, we know that a wage is something we have earned. When we punch the time clock, we expect to be compensated for our time. Paul tells us that, because of who we are, what we produced in our life will result in receiving our just reward or payment. However, what we have earned is death. In short, we sin because we are sinners. It's because of who we are that we receive this wage, not what we do. What may trip us up even more is our understanding of gifts.

We are familiar with receiving and giving gifts on special occasions. Birthdays, anniversaries, Christmas, all of these are days when we expect to receive a gift of some sort. Think for a moment how many of these gifts were actually expected. We make our requests or answer the usual question posed during these special days; "What do you want for...?" There is even an unstated implication of reciprocity. If I receive a gift, I have to give one in return. When was the last time you received a present from someone just because?

That's grace! No special day initiates the gift giving, but you receive a present you neither asked for nor expected to get. The giver, for whatever reason, just decided they wanted to give you something

> The LORD did not set his love upon you, nor choose you, because ye were more in number than any people; for ye were the fewest of all people. Deuteronomy 7:7 KJV

But like the nation of Israel, we forget the true meaning of grace. *We are blessed not because of what we do or who we are, but God blesses us because of who He is and what He has done.*

We often find ourselves trying to justify what God had done because, deep down, we have this sense of unworthiness. Within each person is a "pocket of unworthiness" that finds security in the actions we take. On the surface, we realize that without God and His grace, there is no conceivable way to be "saved."

But our experiences in the world often shape our view of God. We are conditioned to work for things. We try to appease that sense of unworthiness when we give back, usually in the form of keeping the law.

But God's grace isn't based on what we do before or after Christ. With this sense of unworthiness gnawing at our souls, we load ourselves up with do's and don'ts to appease this feeling. However, this is completely opposite God's desire.

In burnt offerings and sacrifices for sin thou hast had
no pleasure. Hebrews 10:6 KJV

We weren't worthy to receive the gift from God. Nevertheless,
we have been given the opportunity to live a life that no amount of
adhering to rules or regulations could give us.

For when you were slaves of sin, you were free in regard
to righteousness. Therefore what benefit were you
then deriving from the things of which you are now
ashamed? For the outcome of those things is death. But
now having been freed from sin and enslaved to God,
you derive your benefit, resulting in sanctification, and
the outcome, eternal life. Romans 6:20-22

Grace freed us from sin. What we could not do ourselves, God
has done through Christ. This gift of grace doesn't stop when we
receive Jesus; in fact, this gift grows in our spirit.

For what the law could not do, in that it was weak
through the flesh, God sending his own Son in the
likeness of sinful flesh, and for sin, condemned sin in
the flesh: That the righteousness of the law might be
fulfilled in us, who walk not after the flesh, but after
the Spirit. Romans 8:3-4 KJV (italics mine)

The weakness of the law has and will always be humanity
and our inability to follow these laws. The law is often used as a
measuring stick to see just how holy we are and, when we fall short,
condemnation awaits. God wants us to live as free people unburdened
by regulations. Living in this burdened state places us in danger of
becoming a slave to works, which biblically means the law, which
points us back to the sin which traps us. This is what the Apostle Paul
calls being slaves to sin. Grace through faith in Jesus Christ gives us
the opportunity to become slaves to righteousness.

But those nagging thoughts persist and teachings abound about the necessity of keeping the laws.

For untold years, humanity has struggled with our innermost thoughts. Often, these inside feelings guide our outside actions. Because of injuries done to us along the way, we respond to situations from these wounds. Grace frees us to live a life by God's power. But this is not an act of will; it is an exchange that Christ makes with us.

To understand grace, we should examine the word atonement as understood by the people of the Old Testament and what atonement after the cross means to New Testament believers.

ATONEMENT

In the Old Testament, the word atonement is used 80 times and always in conjunction with a sacrifice people made. In the Old Testament, the system of sacrifice God instituted told the people when and for what reason they should offer their sacrifices. Every offering was meant to atone for their wrongdoings. But these sacrifices weren't enough; they merely put off the inevitable, which was having their wrong actions place them again at the altar of sacrifice.

In the New Testament (KJV), the word atonement is used only once. Paul used this word when he wrote to the believers in Rome:

> For if, when we were enemies, we were reconciled to God by the death of his Son, much more, being reconciled, we shall be saved by his life. And not only so, but we also joy in God through our Lord Jesus Christ, by whom we have now received the atonement. Romans 5:10-11 KJV

In the Old Testament, the word atonement always meant to cover; when Paul used it in the New Testament, it meant to exchange.

See the difference? To cover something means that what was done probably will turn up again.

When we exchange something, whatever it may be, that item is out of our possession.

To carry this idea further, our actions (following the law) can only cover the wrongs. This is why a yearly sacrifice was required under the Old Covenant. Jesus, by grace, takes away our wrongdoings forever.

It is truly an exchange made on our behalf. The Old Testament model of atonement was what we did; the New Testament model is what Jesus Christ has done!

LAW AND GRACE

> For the law having a shadow of good things to come, and not the very image of the things, can never with those sacrifices which they offered year by year continually make the comers thereunto perfect. Hebrews 10:1 KJV

The law was always pointing us to the grace of God. When properly understood, we know we can't have grace without the law, and to try and bypass the law to grace is a license to sin. Paul's answer to the thought that because of grace we are free to sin was, "God forbid!" Paul gives us clear understanding in scripture about how the law and grace should work in our lives.

> Therefore, my brethren, you also were made to die to the Law through the body of Christ, so that you might be joined to another, to Him who was raised from the dead, in order that we might bear fruit for God. For while we were in the flesh, the sinful passions, which were aroused by the Law, were at work in the members of our body to bear fruit for

> death. But now we have been released from the Law,
> having died to that by which we were bound, so that
> we serve in newness of the Spirit and not in oldness
> of the letter. Roman 7: 4-6

The law was a thing. Grace is a person, Jesus Christ. He is called the grace of God all through the New Testament. It's easy to embrace grace as a philosophy and never embrace grace as a person. The only way to embrace the law is to submit to all the regulations and hope we can keep all that is written. When we submit to grace in the person of Jesus Christ He keeps us! *We are not free to sin, but free from sin!*

The problem? To be found worthy in the eyes of God requires us to be sin-free. The Bible is clear that light and darkness can't be in the same place at the same time.

The answer? Jesus Christ. When God gave Him to us, He gave the only acceptable offering: perfection. When we accept this perfect offering, we then take on the identity of Christ. *God no longer looks at me as a sinner, but a blood-bought saint.*

To say we as believers are holy may sound boastful, but it is this truth that is contained in scripture. Many of Paul's letters were addressed to the "saints" of whatever particular church to which he was writing. What we should know is that the word "saint" and "holy" in the Greek are the same word. In fact, read through the New Testament and see how fitting it is to replace the word saint with the word holy. While we were sinners saved by grace, after the cross on Calvary we are blood-bought saints, which means holy! This should radically change our lives.

We don't need to be held in bondage to our flesh, which naturally will default to keeping rules; it doesn't take faith to keep the law. But because of the finished work of Jesus, we are His people. Our identity is in Him, not us. When we try to find our identity in ourselves we fall short every time.

THE BATTLE WITHIN

> For I know that in me (that is, in my flesh,) dwelleth
> no good thing: for to will is present with me; but how
> to perform that which is good I find not. For the good
> that I would I do not: but the evil which I would not,
> that I do. Romans 7:18-19 KJV

Paul describes in Romans a battle faced by all of humanity, even those who have received Christ; the battle of spirit and flesh. The flesh, our natural nature, as described by Paul without Christ, will always default to doing things that please us first. Think of how a small child reacts when playing with other small children and their playmate takes one of their toys. Usually the response from the child who has the toy taken is, "Mine!" We don't learn these selfish behaviors; we are born with them. These selfish desires cause us and others around us pain.

From an early age, I battled with an addition to alcohol. Even while attending church in my teenage years, the battle raged. After I left the church, I tried to quit on my own. Meetings, abstinence and even living like a hermit failed to fix my drinking problem.

When I met Christ, my life changed, and with this change came the freedom from alcohol. This didn't happen because I focused on my problem of drinking, but because I embraced the promises of Christ. My focus turned to Him, not my problems. The more we focus on our problems, the more likely we will relapse. I'm thankful God freed me from this harmful habit that permeates our church culture.

Think for a moment of a battle you may be facing. *Are you preparing for a battle instead of celebrating victory?* God's grace puts the focus on Him and takes it off of us. As long as we focus on how bad we are, we'll never get better. From the beginning of time, we read in the Bible that humanity was the problem and God was the solution. To focus on our faults only serves to place us back under the condemnation from which we are freed. Remember that was the purpose of the law: to condemn us. As long as we look for hope in our actions, we will never find the victory we seek.

THE SEARCH FOR SIGNIFICANCE

The Bible tells us the reaction of God when He had to banish His most loved creation from the garden. But noticeably absent is the reaction of Adam and Eve that day. The only reaction recorded was how Adam blamed God for giving Him the woman who started the whole mess.

> And the man said, The woman whom thou gavest to
> be with me, she gave me of the tree, and I did eat.
> Genesis 3:12 KJV

In paintings depicting the Fall in the garden that day, we often see Adam and Eve, downtrodden in their appearance as they walk from the garden, covered in animal skins, out of the presence of God. In Genesis Chapter 4, the Bible tells us that Adam and Eve conceived two sons. This well-known story of two brothers has a tragic ending that many who have read the Bible are familiar with. Cain kills his brother Abel.

According to the scripture, Abel brought the "first" from his flock and Cain brought his offering from his crop. God found pleasure from Abel's offering, but Cain's offering He wouldn't even consider. Cain was more than a little upset. Some take this account to mean that Abel's offering was more acceptable because it came from the first offspring of his flock whereas Cain's wasn't. There is an underlying meaning to what was going on here.

Just a few years after the garden was declared off-limits, Cain was scratching a living from the ground God had cursed. Abel chose the pastoral vocation. Cain was tilling the ground and wresting an existence from something cursed while Abel was herding animals.

Consider that it is most likely Abel's "offerings" were eating from Cain's offerings, which, by much effort, were being harvested from the cursed ground.

It was difficult for me to identify with Cain, until I realized that Cain was faced with the same predicament many of us are faced with today. Many of us have been passed over for promotions, declined the recognition we know we should receive. Often our greatest achievements go unheralded. Cain worked hard to produce, and in the presence of God, his efforts weren't acknowledged.

The search for significance began only one generation after the fall. While we may never murder our brother physically, in our minds we feel slighted and secretly rejoice when those who receive what we want for ourselves meet with adversity.

God warned Cain about the danger of the search for significance:

> If thou doest well, shalt thou not be accepted? and if thou
> doest not well, sin lieth at the door. Genesis 4:7 KJV

The sin crouching at the door, for many of us, is the need to be valued and have the assurance that we matter. However, try as we may, this "need" is just out of our grasp. It was just out of Cain's grasp too, and what resulted was the first murder in the history of mankind. We may never take the drastic step that Cain took, but in our minds the deed has already been done. Jesus alluded to this point in Matthew 5 when He made the bold statement:

> Ye have heard that it was said by them of old time, Thou
> shalt not kill; and whosoever shall kill shall be in danger
> of the judgment: But I say unto you, That whosoever
> is angry with his brother without a cause shall be in
> danger of the judgment. Matthew 5:21-22 KJV

Have you ever been angry at someone? Many times, these angry thoughts find their origins in our search for significance. When wronged, we feel the need to stand up for ourselves. But according to Jesus, these thoughts are no different than the actual deed.

Think for a moment of how our need to be valued reveals itself in our lives. We personalize our clothes. We place our names on trophies and hang certificates of accomplishments on our walls. We have personalized license plates and our names on our office doors. When we live by the law and all its demands, our records of good deeds and accomplishments fulfill our need for significance, at least temporarily. Human nature apart from Christ will always default to this need. To those who want to continue to fulfill this need apart from God's grace, Jesus gives an answer.

> And if thy right eye offend thee, pluck it out, and cast it from thee: for it is profitable for thee that one of thy members should perish, and not that thy whole body should be cast into hell. And if thy right hand offend thee, cut it off, and cast it from thee: for it is profitable for thee that one of thy members should perish, and not that thy whole body should be cast into hell. Matthew 5:29-30 KJV

Is Jesus recommending self-mutilation? Should we just try harder to not be angry when someone undermines our sense of worth? Hardly.

Jesus' words show us the impossibility of living the way God intends for us to live without the divine intervention of God. If we want to live by the law, Jesus tells us how. For those who want more rules, Jesus gives more rules. If you insist on taking actions to avoid sin, it will be a painful and miserable experience. For those who recognize the need for God's grace, the cross is where the grace of God is extended to all of humanity. Grace changes everything!

Chapter 5

A New Way

And you, being dead in your sins and the uncircumcision of your flesh, hath he quickened together with him, having forgiven you all trespasses; Blotting out the handwriting of ordinances that was against us, which was contrary to us, and took it out of the way, nailing it to his cross; Colossians 2:13-14 KJV

This past summer, I traveled with my parents to visit my aunt and uncle who live in Florida. My parents have a motor home that is comfortable but a handful on the road, so I volunteered to drive. Over the last twenty-three years, my wife and I have driven that route numerous times - so many times in fact, that I no longer use a map.

While traveling with my parents, I drove this same route with one difference. On the dashboard was a little piece of technology that I had used in the past for other trips, but never used on any trips to Florida. These devices, if programed correctly, will put you at the front door of your destination. The common name for these little marvels of technology is GPS, but there are numerous other brand names.

As we drove through Tennessee, the GPS advised us to exit the interstate we were traveling on and take a new road I had never traveled. But because I was unsure if the address I entered into the unit was correct, I ignored the new directions and continued in the direction I had been many times before. These pieces of technology are great, but they rely on the competence of the user. Enter the wrong address and you will end up at the wrong destination.

What I discovered when I arrived at my aunt and uncle's house that if I would have taken the new direction the GPS provided, our trip would have been about two hours shorter.

Our spiritual lives are much like that. We have a well-worn path of living and interacting with God in a way that we have come to trust. But what if we are experiencing what happened to my parents and me on our trip to Florida? What if God's direction for us is different than our customary route? When the full revelation of grace was revealed to me in scripture, my first reaction was stay on the same course I had always traveled. Much like my trip to Florida, I would eventually arrive at my destination, but God was offering a better way.

In the New Testament, Paul traveled about the region sharing with many Jewish believers the gospel. This gospel was, to some, so blasphemous and contrary to what they had been taught that Paul was often stoned and beaten. Crowds of Jews that held firmly to the law and all its requirements contended with Paul's message of grace and Jesus Christ's sacrifice.

The people of Paul's time found security in the laws and statutes of the Old Testament. Even today, many people unknowingly find their security in the law. The well-worn path of law keeping by their will keeps God's grace at arm's length, still giving power to sin.

Like those people in Paul's time, I used the law, specifically the Ten Commandments, as a measuring stick of holiness rather than a guide as it was intended. However, unlike those people of Paul's time, my introduction to these laws came only after I received Christ. It seemed the longer I was a believer, the more I heard about these laws and the need to keep the law, even though grace saved me.

Instead of letting God's grace transform me, the do's and don'ts of the law became a well-worn path for me. My life looked better, but inside I was struggling to maintain this holy life. It seemed the harder I tried, the harder it was. Finally, I reached the end of my rope; I had had enough! I remember asking God, "What is happening with me? Am I missing something?" Enter the message of grace.

From the vantage point grace provided, I realized God's new way of living life in the kingdom didn't require me to keep every law, nor did I completely throw out the laws. Quite the contrary, actually; because of grace, I no longer fell into the rut of just keeping the laws. Instead, the commandments became promises to embrace. From this new way comes a radically different understanding.

> Having therefore, brethren, boldness to enter into the holiest by the blood of Jesus, By a *new and living way*, which he hath consecrated for us, through the veil, that is to say, his flesh; Hebrews 10:19-20 KJV (italics mine)

By traveling this well-worn path of trying to keep the law to access God's presence, we find that the law keeps us out of His presence if we fall short. The law acts much like the curtain that separated the people from the Holy Place in the temple. But the temple curtain that once kept people from God's presence was ripped away. The commandments once used as a standard of holiness no longer apply because our holiness is found in Jesus, not the laws.

To explain this concept further, let's look at the Ten Commandments, particularly the fourth commandment. The Pharisees often accused Jesus of breaking the Sabbath. But what Jesus shows us in Scripture is that merely keeping the Sabbath, as the Pharisees religiously did, can become one of those well-worn paths.

By His grace we can, indeed, see a new and living way.

THE TEN COMMANDMENTS

1. You shall have no other Gods before me.
2. You shall not make for yourself any carved image
3. You shall not take the name of the Lord your God in vain
4. **Remember the Sabbath day, to keep it holy.**
5. Honor your father and your mother,
6. You shall not murder.
7. You shall not commit adultery.
8. You shall not steal.
9. You shall not bear false witness against your neighbor.
10. You shall not covet

The Ten Commandments are pretty straightforward. Most of us usually have little problem keeping the majority of these laws. But of all the Ten Commandments, the commandment the modern church actually encourages us to break is the fourth commandment.

The Sabbath of the Ten Commandments is specifically the seventh day, which is Saturday. What, then, is our answer when asked, why don't we keep the Sabbath? If we kept the Sabbath, wouldn't that mean that our church services would be held on Saturday?

Many have proposed different answers. The most popular answer is that, since we are under a new covenant, the old rules and regulations from the old covenant are null and void. There is a vague understanding of Christ's fulfillment of the law. But can we find scripture that supports this answer? And if the fourth commandment has been done away with, then what about the other nine? There seems to be a special exemption in place for that particular commandment that doesn't apply to the others.

Many years ago, when I first started attending church, Sunday service became a well-worn path. I never questioned why we held service on Sunday instead of Saturday. I just accepted that was how things were. After all, many people I greatly respected went to church on Sunday. They had been believers longer than I, so for many years, I never questioned this logic. Looking back, I now realize that God was telling me to shut off my GPS.

As I began searching through scriptures, it became obvious that as Jesus performed miracles on the Sabbath, the religious elite took notice. In fact, these people challenged the actions of Jesus, not because He performed miracles, but because He performed them on that holy day.

> And a man was there whose hand was withered. And they questioned Jesus, asking, "Is it lawful to heal on the Sabbath?"--so that they might accuse Him. And He said to them, "What man is there among you who has a sheep, and if it falls into a pit on the Sabbath, will he not take hold of it and lift it out? "How much more valuable then is a man than a sheep! So then, it is lawful to do good on the Sabbath." Then He said to the man, "Stretch out your hand!" He stretched it out, and it was restored to normal, like the other. Matthew 12:10-13

These people even went as far as to question Jesus' disciples when they went through the fields gathering food for a meal.

> Now it happened that He was passing through some grainfields on a Sabbath; and His disciples were picking the heads of grain, rubbing them in their hands, and eating the grain. But some of the Pharisees said, "Why do you do what is not lawful on the Sabbath?" Luke 6:1-2

When confronted by these people with questions about the Sabbath, Jesus gave a simple but profound answer:

> And he said unto them, The sabbath was made for man, and not man for the sabbath: Therefore the Son of man is Lord also of the Sabbath. Mark 2:27-28 KJV

The Sabbath was never intended to become a burden for humanity. It was a day set apart for man's rest. During this day, man would devote himself completely to God and His provision in our lives. Jesus actually states that the Sabbath was for humanity's benefit, not God's. Focusing on the letter of the law ignored the spirit in which the Sabbath was given. God wanted to meet with humanity in a special way, on a special day.

Church on Sunday mornings, for many, is a time such as this. Our weeks are filled with busyness. We need to recuperate and spend time with God and God's people. But this still doesn't answer the question of why our church services are held Sundays instead of Saturdays.

The reason we hold service on Sunday originates on resurrection morning. Jesus came out of the tomb on the day after the Sabbath, which was Sunday. Sunday became a day of celebration because of the victory we have in the finished work of Jesus Christ. In scripture, we have several examples of believers gathering on Sunday:

> And upon the first day of the week, when the disciples came together to break bread, Paul preached unto them, ready to depart on the morrow; and continued his speech until midnight. Acts 20:7 KJV

> Now concerning the collection for the saints, as I have given order to the churches of Galatia, even so do ye. Upon the first day of the week let every one of you lay by him in store, as God hath prospered him, that there be no gatherings when I come. 1 Corinthians 16:1-2 KJV

> I was in the Spirit on the Lord's day, and heard behind
> me a great voice, as of a trumpet, Revelation 1:10 KJV

But none of this completely explains why we don't keep the Sabbath on Saturday. There was never a decree from God to change days of worship. Think about how many people break the Sabbath commandment because of church members gathering at restaurants after church service for a meal. If we were under the law then not only would we be responsible for breaking the Sabbath commandment, but we would be encouraging others to do so as well. Think of all the waitresses, waiters, cashiers and managers that are there to serve us, not to mention the convenient store attendants and television crews who broadcast our football and baseball games during our "restful Sabbath." We will not find the answer we are looking for from the law; only grace explains the change:

> Let us therefore fear, lest, a promise being left us of entering into his rest, any of you should seem to come short of it. For unto us was the gospel preached, as well as unto them: but the word preached did not profit them, not being mixed with faith in them that heard it. For we which have believed do enter into rest, as he said, As I have sworn in my wrath, if they shall enter into my rest: although the works were finished from the foundation of the world. For he spake in a certain place of the seventh day on this wise, And God did rest the seventh day from all his works. And in this place again, If they shall enter into my rest. Seeing therefore it remaineth that some must enter therein, and they to whom it was first preached entered not in because of unbelief: Again, he limiteth a certain day, saying in David, To day, after so long a time; as it is said, Today if ye will hear his voice, harden not your hearts. For if *Jesus* had given them

rest, then would he not afterward have spoken of another day. There remaineth therefore a rest to the people of God. For he that is entered into his rest, he also hath ceased from his own works, as God did from his. 11Let us labor therefore to enter into that rest, lest any man fall after the same example of unbelief. Hebrews 4:1-11 KJV (Italics mine)

Throughout this book I have chosen to use the King James Version of the Bible, as well as The New American Standard Bible. For many years, I was told that the King James Version of the Bible was the only version of the Bible we should read as believers. I won't go into all the different explanations given by those who hold to the idea that The King James Version of the Bible is the best. Instead, let's read that same passage in the New American Standard Bible and compare both:

Therefore, let us fear if, while a promise remains of entering His rest, any one of you may seem to have come short of it. For indeed we have had good news preached to us, just as they also; but the word they heard did not profit them, because it was not united by faith in those who heard. For we who have believed enter that rest, just as He has said, "As I swore in My wrath, They shall not enter My rest," although His works were finished from the foundation of the world. For He has said somewhere concerning the seventh day: "And God rested on the seventh day from all His works"; and again in this passage, "They shall not enter My rest." Therefore, since it remains for some to enter it, and those who formerly had good news preached to them failed to enter because of disobedience, He again fixes a certain day, "Today," saying through David after so long a time just as has been said before, "Today if you hear His voice, Do not harden your hearts. "For if *Joshua* had given them rest, He would not have spoken of another day after that. So there remains a Sabbath rest for the people of God. For the one who has entered His rest has himself also rested from his works, as God did from His. Therefore let us be diligent to enter that rest, so that no one will fall, through following the same example of disobedience. Hebrews 4:1-11 (italics mine)

The passages above tell the story of the children of Israel and their time spent wandering in the wilderness. God had provided the Israelites a place of rest in the Promised Land, but the Israelites wouldn't take what was already given to them because of the report the spies gave the people upon their return. During their exploration, the spies saw giants and became afraid to enter the land, so God banished them to the wilderness. These were the people the writer of Hebrews referred to who would not enter in to rest because of unbelief.

Notice in verse eight the translators of the King James Version use the name Jesus. The Hebrew name, Joshua, is the name Jesus in the Greek. It's unclear as to why the translators of the King James Version chose to use the name Jesus instead of Joshua. But when we insert the name Joshua, as did the translators of the New American Standard Bible, things become clear.

Over the years, as I have read the Bible, God has revealed many truths in His word. I have spent most of my life studying the King James Version. Most of the study materials available to us are from the King James Version. But what I discovered as I sought to understand the meaning of the Sabbath was that, because of the language of the King James Version, I missed some things that would have shed light on my understanding of grace. But let me emphatically state I don't place the blame for my lack of understanding certain truths, like why we don't keep the Sabbath, on the translators of the Bible or on my many teachers. It was me. Just reading the Bible and never asking God to show me what He is saying had become one of those well-worn paths.

The answer to the question of why we don't "keep the Sabbath" is found here in the letter to the Hebrews.

> Let us therefore fear, lest, a promise being left us of entering into his rest, any of you should seem to come short of it. For unto us was the gospel preached, as well as unto them: but the word preached did not profit them, not being mixed with faith in them that heard it. *For we which have believed do enter into rest*, as he said, As I have sworn in my wrath, if they shall enter into my rest: although the works were finished from the foundation of the world. For he spake in a certain place of the seventh day on this wise, And God did rest the seventh day from all his works. And in this place again, If they shall enter into my rest. Hebrews 4:1-5 KJV (italics mine)

Numbers hold great meaning in the Bible and, in the Jewish culture, numbers explained what words often could not. The number seven represents completion. This is the Sabbath day, which was set apart by God because He had "finished" the work of creating the world. *When God told Adam to keep the Sabbath, He was inviting him into His already completed work.* But because of the sin committed in the garden, this Sabbath communion was broken.

> There remaineth therefore a rest to the people of God. For he that is entered into his rest, he also hath ceased from his own works, as God did from his. Hebrews 4:9-10 KJV

> Thus the heavens and the earth were completed, and all their hosts. By the seventh day God completed His work which He had done, and He rested on the seventh day from all His work which He had done. Then God blessed the seventh day and sanctified it, because in it He rested from all His work which God had created and made. Genesis 2:1-3

Think for a moment what exactly Adam did during the creation. What did Adam do to add to God's creation? What did Adam create? God blessed and set apart that day of rest, and Adam reaped the benefit of the accomplished work of the creator. Adam didn't rest from his work, but instead would work from his rest. He followed his first day of life with a day of rest. Adam did nothing to gain that rest; he simply trusted in God's word.

When Jesus spoke the words "it is finished," He fulfilled the requirements of all the laws. When we give our lives to Him we have entered the Sabbath rest. Our work is done in Christ and nothing we can do by keeping laws will add to the finished work of Christ. We no longer keep the Sabbath lawfully by the letter, but by His Spirit that lives in us, we are always at rest in Him. *The Sabbath is not a day we keep, but a new life we are given.*

It was from this understanding Paul shared His message of grace with the churches. His message was simple: stop working for what God has already given you. There is a new way. This new way has nothing to do with special days or our actions.

> One person regards one day above another, another regards every day alike. Each person must be fully convinced in his own mind. He who observes the day, observes it for the Lord, and he who eats, does so for the Lord, for he gives thanks to God; and he who eats not, for the Lord he does not eat, and gives thanks to God. Romans 14:5-6

> Let no man therefore judge you in meat, or in drink, or in respect of an holyday, or of the new moon, or of the Sabbath days: Which are a shadow of things to come; but the body is of Christ. Colossians 2:16-17 KJV

As Paul traveled around the region, he often met with contention on the topic of law and grace. Many of the churches he started were of Jewish descent and, in time, fell back into the old ways rather than accepting the promises of God. The well-worn path of just keeping the laws felt much safer than embracing, by faith, the reality of the completed work of Christ.

> You foolish Galatians, who has bewitched you, before whose eyes Jesus Christ was publicly portrayed as crucified? This is the only thing I want to find out from you: *did you receive the Spirit by the works of the Law, or by hearing with faith?* Are you so foolish? *Having begun by the Spirit, are you now being perfected by the flesh?* Did you suffer so many things in vain--if indeed it was in vain? So then, does He who provides you with the Spirit and works miracles among you, do it by the works of the Law, or by hearing with faith? Galatians 3:1-5 (italics mine)

Throughout the New Testament, Paul challenged the actions of those people who found salvation in Christ through grace, then returned to the well-worn path of keeping the laws to gain the righteousness they already had in Christ.

On my trip to Florida, there was an inner struggle that pulled me in two different directions. One was a well-worn path I traveled many times. I knew that at the end of my travels, I would arrive at the destination I wanted because I was familiar with the way. The other direction provided the opportunity of a shorter, easier path. But I opted to shut off the GPS unit and continue along the same route

I had traveled many times before. I realized that this was the state of my spiritual journey: I was walking a well-worn familiar path that seemed safe, but difficult. I would arrive at my destination, but the journey in no way resembled the life promised in scripture to those who follow Jesus. Unlike my trip to Florida, where I continued down the same path, I chose, by His grace, a new way.

When we meet Christ, there is a newness we have never experienced because it isn't of this world. It's new; it's fresh; it is life-changing.

God has opened through His Spirit the possibility of living above this world while still being in this world. The newness often fades because we are given an incomplete message. Many believers started this new life and, along the way, were told that now that we are Christians, we have to clean up our act! While it is true our lives should look different, this difference is because we reflect Christ, not because we have to act like Him. Reread the words of Paul:

> Are ye so foolish? having begun in the Spirit, are ye
> now made perfect by the flesh? Galatians 3:3 KJV

Like in the lives of many people I have met, legalism and laws overtook what God started for those believers in the Churches of Galatia. The new way Christ promised and Paul preached became lost and misinterpreted. But Paul wasn't the only one spreading this news. Peter was also sharing in the work of proclaiming God's grace:

> Who his own self bare our sins in his own body on
> the tree, that we, being dead to sins, should live unto
> righteousness: by whose stripes ye were healed. 1
> Peter 2:24 KJV

Peter resoundingly affirmed the message of grace Paul shared. The words used by Peter are past tense, meaning "it is finished."

> For Christ also hath once suffered for sins, the just
> for the unjust, that he might bring us to God, being
> put to death in the flesh, but quickened by the Spirit:
> 1 Peter 3:18 KJV

God's grace gives us a new identity. Jesus' sacrifice brought us that grace. Our status has changed from slaves of sin to children of the King.

Jesus shared this promise with the disciples just before He was led to His death on a cross:

> And the glory which thou gavest me I have given
> them; that they may be one, even as we are one:
> John 17:22 KJV

As I read those words, I am humbled. The Savior of the world, the Lamb of God, Creator of heaven and earth, willingly passes on His glory to you and me. His selfless sacrifice benefited only you and me. He had nothing to gain and everything to lose. By His grace, we have a new identity. For many, the complete gift of grace still awaits. It seems too good to be true.

> These shall make war with the Lamb, and the Lamb
> shall overcome them: for he is Lord of lords, and King
> of kings: and they that are with him are called, and
> chosen, and faithful. Revelation 17:14 KJV

From an early age, I knew the Bible referred to Jesus as the King of kings, but it wasn't until I understood the message of grace that I grasped the depth of that passage. Jesus is called the King of kings not only because He has authority and dominion over all earthly kings or rulers, but He is King of those who have embraced their kingship Jesus passed to them. This describes anyone who is saved by the grace of God.

A king lives like a king. A king realizes the power and authority he has because of his position in the kingdom. This new way promises authority and power. This new way guarantees victory and peace. Grace really does change everything.

Chapter 6

The Cover-Up

For the Law, since it has *only* a shadow of the good things to come *and* not the very form of things, can never, by the same sacrifices which they offer continually year by year, make perfect those who draw near. Hebrews 10:1

Around my house, we don't observe the normal rules of etiquette many people follow when cleaning their house. That's not to say we don't clean; in fact, because of the number of people from our church family coming and going, we often clean every day. We have to maintain this standard not only because of the amount of people we have over, but because we have pets that tend to shed. If left unattended for more than a day or two, the furniture grows fur!

Many people clean their houses in the same manner. But for a moment, think about what we do with the dust and dirt and, in our case, animal hair, we sweep from the floors or clean from the furniture. We throw it away! But how much easier would it be if we just swept that dust and dirt under a conveniently placed piece of furniture? We could quadrant up our rooms, throw whatever is near the couch under the couch and maybe slide some under a table. We could even sweep everything else under a conveniently placed throw rug! We could "clean" our houses in a matter of minutes with half the effort.

The problem, I think we all can agree, is that sooner or later the dust and dirt will work itself from under those hidden places. After a few visits from friends and family, when that dust worked its way from under those places, we would conclude we need a better, more permanent way of dealing with the dirt. This is exactly what God was trying to reveal to humanity through the use of the altar and the sacrificial system in place before Jesus.

> For the Law, since it has only a shadow of the good things to come and not the very form of things, can never, by the same sacrifices which they offer continually year by year, make perfect those who draw near. Otherwise, would they not have ceased to be offered, because the worshipers, having once been cleansed, would no longer have had consciousness of sins? But in those sacrifices there is a reminder of sins year by year. For it is impossible for the blood of bulls and goats to take away sins. Hebrews 10:1-4

Most of us have things in our past that we don't make public knowledge and would prefer that no one find out. Many of our bestselling books and movie productions are centered on this "coverup" theme. In everyday life we can, to some extent, keep things covered, but what about when we stand before a perfect God who knows and sees everything?

I remember, as a child, hearing that all the bad things I did and offenses against others that I had committed were "covered by the blood." At the time, this sounded good. Later in ministry, I spoke that same phrase many times. But the problem of reoccurring sin plagued me and many others that I knew. I just couldn't get things right and, when I fell short, I beat myself up.

Kevin Derby

Does any of this sound familiar to you? Does this scenario play out in your life or the lives of people you know? Something was missing and what was missing was making life tough. Tough enough at times that I would ask myself why would I want to tell anybody about Jesus. What's so great about being a Christian? It seems that all I ever do is mess up and then mess up again. What I discovered through scripture study and prayer changed my life: it all starts and ends with grace.

THE PROBLEM

> For seven days you shall make atonement for the altar and consecrate it; then the altar shall be most holy, and whatever touches the altar shall be holy.
> Exodus 29:37

Most of us today have a difficult time reading about the Old Testament holy days with any deep understanding as to what those special days meant. Without a basic understanding of what those days represented, it becomes a challenge to "unwrap" this gift of grace God offers everyone.

Rosh Hashanah begins the Jewish New Year. This is when the shofar, or ram's horn, is sounded in the temple to herald in the New Year and, with this High Holy sound, comes much celebration. On the tenth day is Yom Kippur, known as the Day of Atonement.

There is richness and beauty in the way those from the Jewish culture observed and still observe these days. In biblical times, there were strict rules of observance for Yom Kippur, called the most Holy of Days. During this time, people would reflect and remember those times when they had committed sins against God and seek forgiveness. People would ask for forgiveness of those sins during this time and would make sacrifices to cover or atone for those sins.

Remember, the Hebrew word atone means "to cover." This covering received from God wasn't permanent. There was a yearly

High Holy Day to secure this covering for Gods people. Why? Because people are people and, left to our own devices, we make mistakes. But this Holy Day served a greater purpose in the lives of humanity. This day showed humanity the need for a permanent solution. Read the passage from Exodus again:

> For seven days you shall make atonement for the altar and consecrate it; then the altar shall be most holy, and whatever touches the altar shall be holy. Exodus 29:37

It's difficult to imagine the elation and sense of rightness with God those people experienced during this time of covering. To a nation that was God's, this meant access to His blessings, freedom from condemnation, and a new start. They were told by God "to be Holy even as I am Holy," and for that time they were. But...

I don't have to finish that sentence because we have all at one time or another had that experience. We sense God's presence in our lives and, for that moment, things are right. For a while, that fresh sense of cleanliness and rightness with God permeates our being. Then life happens. That rightness and oneness with God becomes distorted.

We soon find ourselves back in the same spot as we were before. So what do we do? The same thing the Jewish nation did: revisit that altar to receive that covering. Does any of this sound familiar? Does this sound like "good news?" Or does this seem like we have something dangled in front of us that is just out of our reach? The apostle Paul fielded these sorts of questions many times during his ministry. What would he say? Read on:

> *Dear (your name),* Do this, knowing the time, that it is already the hour for you to awaken from sleep; for now salvation is nearer to us than when we believed. *Paul* (Italics mine). Romans 13:11

The problem we face is this idea of atonement found in the Old Testament isn't a permanent solution. The whole idea of covering something up doesn't have the true gospel ring of finality Jesus promised us from the cross. When Jesus said "it is finished" not only was that a statement from God telling us that Jesus had accomplished His will, but it was also a promise to us. This promise tells us our efforts mean nothing. How can we add to what God has accomplished? It is finished. The covering previously provided has been set aside because Jesus fulfilled the law and its requirements. Many people have difficulty receiving this truth because of what they were taught in the past. But from our source, the Bible, we find the answer to all our problems:

> But now He has obtained a more excellent ministry, by as much as He is also the mediator of a *better covenant*, which has been enacted on better promises. For if that first covenant had been faultless, there would have been no occasion sought for a second. *For finding fault with them,...* Hebrews 8:6-8 (italics mine)

That Jesus fulfilled the requirements of the laws, thereby nullifying the consequences of the law, in no way undermines or cancels the holiness of God-given laws. We do that on our own, "for finding fault with them." The weakness of the law is our inability to keep it. The covering received from sacrifices was never meant to be a permanent answer, but show us the permanence of the problem without Jesus. The sacrifices, the altar and all those rules were always to point humanity to God's grace.

THE SOLUTION

> And not only so, but we also joy in God through our Lord Jesus Christ, by whom we have now received the *atonement.* Romans 5:11 KJV (italics mine)

One of the deepest and most life changing letters ever written by Paul, inspired by God, was the letter to those Roman believers almost 2000 years ago. This letter has changed countless lives and released millions from bondage. As I read this letter over and over in my search to find what I was missing, I came across Romans 5:11 and it radically changed my life.

The Old Testament idea of atonement, or covering, has permeated our Christian culture for two thousand years. This concept has, unaware to us, undermined the power of the Gospel. We spend so much time, energy and money trying to just make life livable and, in doing so, we have settled for second best. The gospel has power and that power comes from God, not from how we try to live it out.

The idea of thousands of people doing good things for God and in His name sounds appealing and almost has a ring of truth to it, but it's a toothless gospel that is destined for failure. Could this be why Jesus made this statement?

> "Not everyone who says to Me, 'Lord, Lord,' will enter the kingdom of heaven, but he who does the will of My Father who is in heaven will enter. "Many will say to Me on that day, 'Lord, Lord, did we not prophesy in Your name, and in Your name cast out demons, and in Your name perform many miracles?'" And then I will declare to them, "I never knew you; depart from Me, you who practice lawlessness." Matthew 7:21-23

I have to admit that statement from Jesus rattled me, because it described me. I pastor at a church; I tend to the needs of the poor; I love my neighbor. Jesus, are you telling me that's not enough? I don't practice lawlessness; in fact, I make sure I cross all the T's and dot all the I's in my do-good checklist! Maybe I need to do more miracles, speak in tongues, walk on water, give everything away, the list goes on.

The answer for me was found in that single passage from Paul. In that verse, Paul uses an Old Testament word that has a new meaning. Under the Old Covenant, atonement was a temporary state that changed as soon as I sinned. I was "covered." But when Paul uses this word, it means something totally different.

If you have a Strong's concordance, look this word up in the King James Version and you'll find this word used one time in the whole New Testament. It means exchange. Now read that passage from Paul with this new definition:

> And not only so, but we also joy in God through our Lord Jesus Christ, by whom we have now received the atonement. *(Exchange)* Romans 5:11 KJV (Italics mine)

The actual root of this word means to mutually change. It means that what I have is given willingly to God, the bad and the good, and Christ gives me what is His. *It's not, and never has been, about living a changed life; it's about an exchanged life!* Think about it this way. Why would Jesus say "it is finished," but leave things undone enough for me to have to complete the work myself? In short, why did Jesus even need to die if there were things I could do in the first place?

What we often fail to recognize, because of errant teaching, is that many of the statements Paul and the other New Testament writers made weren't commands for us to do better. They were fulfilled promises of what Jesus has accomplished in us. Even the Old Testament laws are promises.

If Jesus walked the earth 2000 years ago, kept all the laws and ordinances, and now this same Holy Spirit that lived in Jesus now lives in us, guess what that means? We have that same power available. As Jesus lives His life in us, those laws and ordinances we rebelled against now become blessings. We don't keep any of the laws or do good because we fear a vengeful God, but because Jesus' nature is in us. He took our sin nature to the cross and gave us His nature at the resurrection.

> He made Him who knew no sin *to be* sin on our behalf, so that we might become the righteousness of God in Him. 2 Corinthians 5:21

The word sin in Romans specifically doesn't mean the bad things we do; it means the bad within us. When this heavenly exchange takes place, that nature is now the property of Jesus Christ; I have no right to it! Instead, the Spirit of the Creator of the universe lives in me, with all His power and strength.

> This is the message we have heard from Him and announce to you, that God is Light, and in Him there is no darkness at all. 1 John 1:5

Light and darkness cannot exist in the same place. Not only is this a physical reality, but it is a spiritual truth found in the Bible. Think of it this way. How can we take the dark out of a room? That's right: turn on the light. Darkness, among other things, symbolizes sin. We would never dream of trying to take darkness out of a room! That would be impossible without a power greater than darkness. It's no different with sin.

I spent years living by the laws and trying to "pick" the sin out of my life. I was actually relying on the law to clean up my act with God. But those laws were never intended to do that. I thought faith meant believing those laws were for my good, when actually, in God's eyes, they were meant for just the opposite. The sole purpose of the laws was to show me how I miss the mark. I soon realized that living by the law took very little faith; instead it took a power that was greater than me. No doubt I was convinced that God couldn't occupy the same space as sin; I knew that much, but how to get this problem of sin under control eluded me. The best I could ever hope for was sin management.

SIN MANAGEMENT

Sadly, much of the church lives under the sin management concept. We hear about how far we fall short and are encouraged to do better. My experiences didn't include encouragement, but rather condemnation. This was explained to me as the work of the Holy Spirit convicting me to do right. So my response was to try harder. But try as I might, I sensed that I was nowhere even close to God's standards. In fact, I found myself looking and feeling much like the person Jesus said we would not be in John 14:

> "I will not leave you as orphans; I will come to you."
> John 14:18

No doubt, as the Spirit of God lives in me, things that are sin are revealed to me. However, what I experience is exactly the opposite of condemnation. It's a deeper realization of my wrongdoings. When I humbly present myself before God, I fulfill the promise made to each of us by God as He spoke through the Apostle Paul:

> And he said unto me, My grace is sufficient for thee: for my strength is made perfect in weakness. Most gladly therefore will I rather glory in my infirmities, that the power of Christ may rest upon me. 1 Corinthians 12:9 KJV

As we realize the power to live a life pleasing to God rests only in the finished work of Jesus and not in our own strength, grace awakens in our spirit. I've heard many people claim this passage and then return to doing things their way. But when we humbly acknowledge we can't please God without His help, we are in a perfect position to receive from God what He has promised. It's that spirit of humility Paul speaks of when he wrote to the church at Philippi:

> Have this attitude in yourselves which was also in Christ Jesus, who, although He existed in the form

> of God, did not regard equality with God a thing to
> be grasped, but emptied Himself, taking the form of a
> bond-servant, and being made in the likeness of men.
> Being found in appearance as a man, He humbled
> Himself by becoming obedient to the point of death,
> even death on a cross. Philippians 2:5-8

Jesus humbled Himself from a power source that was greater than anything in this world. This same power is available to any person who accepts the exchanged life. As I began to understand exactly what this exchanged life really looked like, things began to change. I still messed up, but when I did, there was not condemnation. Instead, there was a spiritual awareness that resonated in me which compelled me to make right what I wronged, not from fear of God's judgment, but hunger for His presence. This exchanged life changed everything for me. When God showed this to me, I felt like the weight of the world was lifted off my shoulders. I called my mentor Mark and, through tears of joy, told him that I felt that I had been saved all over again. It's an exchange that allows me to live a life pleasing to God.

In the book of James, we read the words "it is impossible to please God without faith." In the Gospels, we read about Jesus' baptism. The Holy Spirit descended on Him like a dove and a voice came from heaven and said, "This is my son in whom I am well pleased." God was pleased with Jesus, and when we receive Jesus and His promises in faith, guess with whom God is pleased? That's right, us! We are now part of this earthly Kingdom of God that is mobile and walks in power, bringing honor to His name. Jesus is living His life through us and that's all made possible by His grace.

> For by grace you have been saved through faith; and that
> not of yourselves, it is the gift of God. Ephesians 2:8

Grace changes everything!

Chapter 7

Mind Games

As far as the east is from the west, so far hath he removed
our transgressions from us. Psalms 103:12 KJV

The exchanged life Jesus promises is a reality to every believer
in scripture. Not fully realizing this truth seriously hindered
my walk with God for many years. When I accepted this truth, the
change I experienced was immediate. However, as I began to live out
this exchanged life, the enemy bombarded my mind with thoughts
that caused me to question this exchanged life God promises.

Mind games are the enemy's specialty. For this reason, Paul
encourages every believer to put on the full armor of God:

> Put on the whole armor of God, that ye may be able
> to stand against the wiles of the devil. For we wrestle
> not against flesh and blood, but against principalities,
> against powers, against the rulers of the darkness of
> this world, against spiritual wickedness in high places
> Wherefore take unto you the whole armor of God,
> that ye may be able to withstand in the evil day, and
> having done all, to stand. Stand therefore, having
> your loins girt about with truth, and having on the
> breastplate of righteousness; And your feet shod with
> the preparation of the gospel of peace; Above all,

taking the shield of faith, wherewith ye shall be able
to quench all the fiery darts of the wicked. And take
the helmet of salvation, and the sword of the Spirit,
which is the word of God. Ephesians 6:11-17 KJV

All believers everywhere are in a battle. Many "claim" this
passage when trials arise; never fully grasping that Paul encourages
every believer to remain battle ready. Reread Ephesians 6:17:

And take the helmet of salvation, and the sword of the
Spirit, which is the word of God. Ephesians 6:17 KJV

This helmet of salvation is the protection available to every
believer. We don't just put on the helmet of salvation; we keep it on
at all times! The helmet of salvation keeps those thoughts at bay that
may creep in and draw our attention back to the things we have done
or may do instead of resting in the finished work of Christ.

How much more shall the blood of Christ, who
through the eternal Spirit offered himself without
spot to God, purge your conscience from dead works
to serve the living God? Hebrews 9:14 KJV

A guilty conscience will always force us to look over our
shoulder. The cross is behind us and the resurrection is in front of
us, always. To look back past the cross to our sin, is reminiscent of
when Lot's wife looked back and turned into a pillar of salt. While
things done in the past will have earthly consequences, these things
have heavenly forgiveness. To look back at our sin continuously is
deadly!

There is nothing wrong with looking back at our past as long
as that look back is to show us the way things are now. Lot's wife's
thoughts lingered on a land she left behind. As the Bible records
what happened that day, we read that Lot's wife looked back before
the city was destroyed.

Afterwards, Abraham went to a place that overlooked the city after it was destroyed. So it wasn't the look back that made the difference; it was how she viewed the land she left. Abraham viewed the city as a sinful place that had to be destroyed. Lot's wife looked back, past her husband Lot, to see the city she was leaving. Luke quotes Jesus' words and helps us put things in perspective.

> But the same day that Lot went out of Sodom it rained fire and brimstone from heaven, and destroyed them all. Even thus shall it be in the day when the Son of man is revealed. In that day, he which shall be upon the housetop, and his stuff in the house, let him not come down to take it away: and he that is in the field, let him likewise not return back. Remember Lot's wife. Whosoever shall seek to save his life shall lose it; and whosoever shall lose his life shall preserve it. Luke 17: 29-33 KV

It appears that glance back wasn't just a casual look over her shoulder. She was still attached to a life from which God brought her out. Many times, those looks back are shame filled because of sin we had in our lives at the time before we met Jesus. Sin brings shame. If Jesus exchanged our lives with His, then He died for that shame; it's His and we don't even have the right to ask for it back.

Many of us remember the days before the Internet and debit cards. We would purchase our needed items at a store, record the purchase in our check book and then, at the end of the month, receive the canceled checks and reconcile our checkbooks. The checks we received at the month's end usually had a bank stamp that clearly showed the check had been cashed and was no longer valid. Imagine the look on a store clerk's face if we insisted on cashing one of those cancelled checks. Thankfully, God does not hold our cancelled sin and trespasses against us.

> And you, being dead in your sins and the uncircumcision of your flesh, hath he quickened together with him, having forgiven you all trespasses; Blotting out the handwriting of ordinances that was against us, which was contrary to us, and took it out of the way, nailing it to his cross. Colossians 2:13-14 KJV

The enemy will always try to make our fallen past a present reality. His goal is to change our focus from our present state of righteousness, to our past state of sinfulness. But when we grasp the enormity of the gift of grace, it will change our lives forever. Forever is a long time.

> But this man, after he had offered one sacrifice for sins *forever*, sat down on the right hand of God; From henceforth expecting till his enemies be made his footstool. For by one offering he hath perfected *forever* them that are sanctified. Hebrews 10:12-14 KJV (italics mine)

Because of the poetic nature and symbolism often found in scripture, we often read the words found in the Bible and then attach a definition to those words which often falls far short of their intended meaning. For example, take verse 14 of Hebrews Chapter 10:

> For by one offering he hath perfected *forever* them that are sanctified. Hebrews 10:14 KJV (italics mine)

The writer makes it clear from the previous portion of Scripture that one offering is Jesus. He has perfected forever, meaning He has carried out or completed the requirements for *our* perfection. Take that passage at face value. We are perfected and made complete because of His offering forever! No matter what we hear or encounter in life, Jesus has made this process complete in Him. We couldn't, nor will we ever be able to add to, or take away from what He has done on the cross.

Most of us at least partially understand the concept of being saved by grace and that we are helpless to save ourselves. But I wonder if we fully understand that our actions can't take away that same grace. In other words, if we fail to live up to the standards of the Bible, do we somehow fall short again? This is exactly what Paul was addressing to the believers in Galatia:

> Behold, I Paul say unto you, that if ye be circumcised, Christ shall profit you nothing. For I testify again to every man that is circumcised, that he is a debtor to do the whole law. Christ is become of no effect unto you, whosoever of you are justified by the law; ye are fallen from grace. Galatians 5:2-4 KJV

Paul may have been addressing the act of circumcision, but apply his words to our present condition. If we understand that Jesus completed what was needed on our behalf, then nothing we do, or fail to do, changes that truth! Here lies the trouble with our thinking, which has been formed from living in a world that expects performance.

As a child growing up in church, I was taught that God can't look at sin. To some extent, this is true. So the natural response for me, was to try not to sin. After all, if God can't look at sin, then I don't want God to turn His back on me. God becomes a task master that rewards when I get things right and punishes me when I don't.

However, from a practical standpoint, this is an incomplete understanding of the nature of God. If God couldn't look at sin, then practically, how could he have ever looked at a world that needed saving? What many of us have been taught about sin and how God views this sin is completely inaccurate. This incomplete understanding is often used in conjunction with a verse found in the writings of one of the Minor Prophets named Habakkuk:

> Thou art of purer eyes than to behold evil, and canst
> not look on iniquity... Habakkuk 1:13 KJV

Contextually, Habakkuk's statement is directed towards God, questioning how or why God would let a sinful nation, the Chaldeans, conquer His chosen people. Many have taken this passage out of context and applied inaccurate theology to it. The results of this have been disastrous. Other than the words of Jesus on the cross (*Eli, Eli, lama sabachthani?* which translated in English reads: *My God, my God, why hast thou forsaken me?),* nowhere in scripture does the Bible state that God can't look on sin. In fact, from the very beginning of the Bible, we find Him dealing graciously with Adam and Eve after they had eaten the forbidden fruit.

ADAM AND EVE

The very first recipients of grace found in the Bible were our original parents, Adam and Eve. From the very beginning, God and Adam were close. They often walked in the Garden together admiring God's handy work and enjoyed the company of one another. God knew Adam so well that God sensed Adam's loneliness. It was God who recognized Adam's loneliness. So He created another human for Adam's company, Eve.

God knows about community. The Holy Trinity, since before the creation of time, was in perfect communion and, since God had created man in His image, a part of that image was a desire for community.

When the serpent tempted Eve and she ate of the fruit, Adam was at a crossroads. He willingly ate of the fruit Eve gave him.

> And Adam was not deceived, but the woman being
> deceived was in the transgression. 1 Timothy 2:14 KJV

At that very moment sin, or disobedience to God, entered the world. But God's response wasn't what many are often led to believe in our New Testament churches. God did not send worldwide plagues or tsunamis to deal with Adam's sin. Instead, God went on the "hunt" for Adam, and has been ever since.

> And the LORD God called unto Adam, and said unto him, Where art thou? And he said, I heard thy voice in the garden, and I was afraid, because I was naked; and I hid myself. Genesis 3:9-10 KJV

God never turned His eyes away from Adam or refused to listen to him, as is often said in our churches, when we try to explain the doctrine of sin. Instead, *it was Adam who turned away from God.* What we fail to realize, or have been incorrectly taught about how God views us when we sin, has led us down the path of performing for Him. What the Bible teaches us about God shows us that He doesn't turn away from us when we sin; we turn from Him. His flow of grace into our life by His Spirit is cut off. Why? Without faith, it is impossible to please God. We are saved by grace through *faith,* period.

Most of the time sin occurs in our lives because we take the reins and try to do things our way. It is our action that creates a separation from God. Our faith wavers, but God's love towards us never does. There is an interesting passage in Romans that gives great insight as to how faith works in our life:

> Paul, a servant of Jesus Christ, called to be an apostle, separated unto the gospel of God, (Which he had promised afore by his prophets in the holy scriptures), Concerning his Son Jesus Christ our Lord, which was made of the seed of David according to the flesh; And declared to be the Son of God with power, according to the spirit of holiness, by the resurrection from the dead: By whom we have received *grace* and apostleship, for *obedience to the faith* among all nations, for his name. Romans 1:1-5 KJV (italics mine)

Paul clearly states that *from grace came his obedience to the faith.* We are obedient because of our grace-given faith. We usually try to build our faith through obedience. Our faith is of Christ. Our obedience is a natural response to our faith. But we know that we still mess up and, if God's response to sin isn't Him ignoring us or condemning us, what is it? For that, we have to look back into the Garden of Eden:

> They heard the sound of the LORD God walking in the garden in the cool of the day, and the man and his wife hid themselves from the presence of the LORD God among the trees of the garden. *Then the LORD God called to the man, and said to him, "Where are you?"* He said, "I heard the sound of You in the garden, and I was afraid because I was naked; so I hid myself." And He said, "Who told you that you were naked? Have you eaten from the tree of which I commanded you not to eat?" The man said, "The woman whom You gave to be with me, she gave me from the tree, and I ate." Then the LORD God said to the woman, "What is this you have done?" And the woman said, "The serpent deceived me, and I ate." The LORD God said to the serpent, "Because you have done this, Cursed are you more than all cattle, And more than every beast of the field; On your belly you will go, And dust you will eat All the days of your life; And I will put enmity Between you and the woman, And between your seed and her seed; He shall bruise you on the head, And you shall bruise him on the heel." To the woman He said, "I will greatly multiply Your pain in childbirth, In pain you will bring forth children; Yet your desire will be for your husband, And he will rule over you." Then to Adam He said, "Because you have listened to the

85

voice of your wife, and have eaten from the tree about which I commanded you, saying, 'You shall not eat from it'; Cursed is the ground because of you; In toil you will eat of it All the days of your life. "Both thorns and thistles it shall grow for you; And you will eat the plants of the field; By the sweat of your face You will eat bread, Till you return to the ground, Because from it you were taken; For you are dust, And to dust you shall return." Now the man called his wife's name Eve, because she was the mother of all the living. The LORD God made garments of skin for Adam and his wife, and clothed them. Then the LORD God said, "Behold, the man has become like one of Us, knowing good and evil; and now, he might stretch out his hand, and take also from the tree of life, and eat, and live forever"-- therefore the LORD God sent him out from the garden of Eden, to cultivate the ground from which he was taken. So He drove the man out; and at the east of the garden of Eden He stationed the cherubim and the flaming sword which turned every direction to guard the way to the tree of life. Genesis 3:8-24 (italics mine)

God's response to Adam and Eve's sin wasn't to look away or ignore them. Instead, He demanded justice. God sees the sin of the world and it breaks His heart, as it should ours. That day in the garden, a spiritual death occurred, but physical deaths occurred as well.

In verse 21, we read that both Adam and Eve were clothed in animal skins to hide their nakedness. Animals do not willingly give their skins, so their lives were sacrificed that day. Not only were Adam and Eve physically naked before they ate the fruit; spiritually, they were bare before God. That Edenic relationship with God was one of pure openness and honesty. All that was lost in the garden that day Adam and Eve ate the fruit.

To say that God can't look at sin means that while we were sinners, we were off the radar screen of God. From scripture we can plainly see this is not the case.

We see examples of God speaking openly with people who sinned, such as Cain. We also see him talking openly with those who stood in direct contradiction to His words. Consider Jonah. To say that God can't look at sin would mean we have to ignore thousands of years of scripture. Consider this verse in Malachi:

For I am the LORD, I change not. Malachi 3:6

Our understanding of God's view of sin might be the culprit. A more biblically accurate explanation of how God views sin is that He can't and won't approve of sin. This is a far cry from saying that He can't look at sin; to do that would mean He would never consider the state we are in before we received Christ. But just like that day in the garden, the enemy will constantly attack us through our thoughts and, left unchecked, these impure thoughts will results in sinful actions.

WHICH SINS?

When Christ fulfilled all the requirements of the law on the cross that day on Golgotha, He said these words: "It is finished."

This was not only a proclamation Jesus made to God on our behalf but a declaration of independence to the enemy. He was claiming His victory over the power of the devil which had made us his slaves. But we know, first from scripture and secondly from our experience, the enemy won't go away quietly. Misery loves company.

As a child of God, we know when we miss the mark. No one needs to tell us what is right and what is wrong; this happened way back in the garden. Remember, the tree Adam and Eve ate from was the tree of the knowledge of *good and evil*. The fruit eaten gave humanity the ability to distinguish between the two. Consider what Paul told the church at Rome:

> For when the Gentiles, which have not the law, do by nature the things contained in the law, these, having not the law, are a law unto themselves: Which shew the work of the law written in their hearts, their conscience also bearing witness, and their thoughts the mean while accusing or else excusing one another. Romans 2:14-15 KJV

Paul says that those who were raised in Gentile homes know the difference between right and wrong. Even when I was far from God and not living for or with Him, I knew what was right and wrong. The difference in my life now isn't a revelation of this knowledge of sin, but repulsion from sin that I already know about. We are hardwired to know the difference between right and wrong, but God, through His Spirit, gives His people the ability to overcome these sins rather than let sins control them.

In the book of Psalms we read these words:

> The LORD is merciful and gracious, slow to anger, and plenteous in mercy. He will not always chide: neither will he keep his anger forever. He hath not dealt with us after our sins; nor rewarded us according to our iniquities. For as the heaven is high above the earth, so great is his mercy toward them that fear him. As far as the east is from the west, so far hath he removed our transgressions from us. Psalms 103:8-12. KJV

Combine this prophetic proclamation of David with the words of Jesus on the cross and we read in Hebrews (For by one offering He hath perfected forever them that are sanctified. Hebrews 10:14), and we have a true picture of God's grace to those who accept it.

Consider the great distance David is talking about in verse 12. If we leave our house and travel north, we will eventually pass the North Pole. As we pass the North Pole we will begin to follow a southerly trajectory. If we continue to travel south we will then cross the South Pole, where the opposite is true; we begin to travel back north.

Not so when we travel east and west. No matter how far we travel east, we will always travel east. No matter how far we travel west, we will always be heading in a westerly direction. When God says our sins are cast as far as the east is from the west, He is saying they are gone and we will never meet those sins again. Now take this knowledge to the cross. Of which sins has Christ forgiven us?

Remember, He was crucified 2,000 years ago! The answer can only be all *past, present and future sins.* Don't forget that He not only gave Himself for what we have done or will do, but for who we were: sinners. We were sinners because of our sinful nature. We were spiritually dead and needed a rebirth to accomplish His will in our lives.

> And you hath he quickened, who were dead in trespasses and sins; Wherein in time past ye walked according to the course of this world, according to the prince of the power of the air, the spirit that now worketh in the children of disobedience: Among whom also we all had our conversation in times past in the lusts of our flesh, fulfilling the desires of the flesh and of the mind; and were by nature the children of wrath, even as others. But God, who is rich in mercy, for his great love wherewith he loved us, Even when we were dead in sins, hath quickened us together with Christ, (by grace ye are saved;) And hath raised us up together, and made us sit together in heavenly places in Christ Jesus: Ephesians 2:1–6 KJV

But so often we succumb to the teaching of many well-meaning teachers who insist on our confessing each stumble we experience. This constant revisiting of offenses only serves to give voice to the enemy who insists on bombarding our minds with lies of incompetence and the hopelessness of never overcoming those shortcomings. In the book of Revelation, John identifies our enemy and tells us of his tactic:

> And I heard a loud voice saying in heaven, Now is come salvation, and strength, and the kingdom of our God, and the power of his Christ: *for the accuser of our brethren* is cast down, which accused them before our God day and night. Revelation 12:10 (italics mine)

I once met a man who insisted on listing every offense he committed during the day. He would confess in his nightly prayer every sin he committed. Then, just to make sure he didn't miss any sins, he would ask for mercy from God for any sins he had forgotten.

At that time in my faith, I wasn't equipped to show him the error of his thinking, but I hope that someone has shared the gospel message of grace with him. I do, however remember thinking to myself, "What if he died with unconfessed sin in his life? Would God take back His promise of salvation because he died before he could confess these sins? Does God work this way? What if, during the day I sinned and forgot to confess my sin? Would I share the same fate?"

While many of us may not carry the doctrine of sin to this extreme, have you ever wondered why we ask for forgiveness of sins that Christ has already forgiven? After all, from the vantage point of the cross, any sin we would commit would have been placed in the category of "future sin." This created a serious dilemma for me until I understood what repentance was all about in the Kingdom of God.

REPENTANCE

As we read through the Gospels, we find what has become known as the Lord's Prayer.

> After this manner therefore pray ye: Our Father which art in heaven, Hallowed be thy name. Thy kingdom come. Thy will be done in earth, as it is in heaven. Give us this day our daily bread. And forgive us our debts, as we forgive our debtors. And lead us not into temptation, but deliver us from evil: For thine is the kingdom, and the power, and the glory, forever. Amen. Matthew 6: 9-13 KJV

From this passage, many understand that Jesus is telling us to ask forgiveness from God of our sin. As Jesus spoke, he continued teaching about this needed forgiveness.

> For if ye forgive men their trespasses, your heavenly Father will also forgive you: But if ye forgive not men their trespasses, neither will your Father forgive your trespasses. Matthew 6:14-15 KJV

From these passages, many sermons have been taught about the need for forgiveness in our lives from God and others. While the Bible clearly states, in both the Old and New Testaments, we should make amends with those we have wronged, making amends with God in Jesus' time was a different proposition altogether. The law clearly says that forgiveness from God only comes one way. Sacrifices were the only way to atone for all sins against God, period.

> For the life of the flesh is in the blood: and I have given it to you upon the altar to make an atonement for your souls: for it is the blood that maketh an atonement for the soul. Leviticus 17:11 KJV

> And almost all things are by the law purged with
> blood; and without shedding of blood is no remission.
> Hebrews 9:22 KJV

Before Jesus' death and resurrection, it would be impossible to even consider asking for forgiveness from God without a sacrifice and a priest of the temple to oversee this act.

Remember, Jesus was preparing the way for God to set up His earthly kingdom. That was the meaning of His statement, "Thy Kingdom come." This conversation Jesus had with His disciples was before the cross. The Old Covenant was still in place and Jesus was previewing the possibility of forgiveness His death would bring and the impossibility of forgiveness without shedding the blood of sacrifices. This explains the horror of the Pharisees when Jesus made the statement to the cripple man, "your sins are forgiven" (Mark 2:5).

Instead of believers seeking forgiveness, we are saints requiring repentance.

Repentance has often been explained as forgiveness, which is, scripturally, an inaccurate definition. When we are saved, we confess our sin (our inability to live righteously without Christ) and ask forgiveness, then repentance. Repentance is turning away, or changing direction.

What we should experience as believers when we miss the mark is a sense of grief over our actions. This grief comes from a heart that has been reborn to stay in step with God. When we repent, this means we are turning away from what we were doing and aligning our will with God's will. Instead of merely turning from sin, we are turning to God.

> For godly sorrow worketh repentance to salvation
> not to be repented of: but the sorrow of the world
> worketh death. 2 Corinthians 7:10 KJV

The Godly sorrow Paul refers to literally means grief. This grief leads us to repentance. The word repentance, in no way by definition or contextual usage, implies forgiveness. Forgiveness is already ours.

The mind focused on God continuously thinks of godly things. When we focus on those godly things, godly actions will follow. We often underestimate the power of our minds, but Paul doesn't:

> And be not conformed to this world: but be ye transformed by the renewing of your mind, that ye may prove what is that good, and acceptable, and perfect, will of God. Romans 12:2 KJV

To do the will of God means to make the choices God makes. It is a mind that is constantly immersed in the word of God and, by this immersion, is constantly aware of God and His presence in our lives. The enemy will always be there to trip us up. He won't quit. His weapons of choice are those thoughts of inadequacy and spiritual ineptness. But God gave us a powerful weapon against these attacks. This weapon is a complete and thorough understanding of whose we are, no matter what happens and how bad we mess up.

Grace changes everything, even the way we think, forever!

Chapter 8

The Altar and the Cross

> We have an altar, whereof they have no right to eat which serve the tabernacle. Hebrews 13:10 KJV

So much of how we live today as believers is muddled and mixed with incomplete understanding and confusion. Much of what is said in Any Church, USA sounds good, but when we hold these incomplete teachings up to the true light of scripture, there are contradictions. These contradictions often lead to mass confusion in the church. When we read in scripture one thing and see something different during our church services, confusion will ultimately ensue.

Take for example, the altar and the cross. In the Old Testament, we become very familiar with the altar. After disembarking from the ark with his family, Noah built an altar. Fast forward to Abraham, the father of the Jewish nation, and we find him doing the same thing many times in the Old Testament scriptures. In fact, all the people whose lives were highlighted in the Old Testament were found, at one time or another, sacrificing at the altar. The Israelites weren't the only people that sacrificed at the altar. Pagans used these altars in "high places" to carry out their sacrifices to their pagan gods as well.

The word altar, at its root, means slaughter. This concept escapes us. Most of us nowadays live in societies where our food and all other needed items are gathered for us. If we want a hamburger, we usually buy a pack of hamburger meat from the grocery store. The whole process of killing the animal and preparing the meat is done out of our sight.

In many churches, we have a place at the front of the church called the altar. This is where many who wish to give their lives to Jesus are called together to pray and receive their salvation. The problem with this scenario is what the altar represented. In the days of Noah, Abraham, and Moses, and even up to the times of Jesus, the altar was a sacred place nonbelievers were not allowed to approach.

The temple altar in Jerusalem was so sacred, that it was off-limits to anyone who wasn't a priest. The temple itself was sectioned off into two quadrants: the gentile's court, where Jesus turned over the tables of the money changers, and the court of Israel which was off-limits to gentiles (non-Jewish people). There was said to be a sign displayed prominently which stated "gentiles enter upon penalty of death". The idea of letting a person who was not specifically appointed to this task of sacrificing at the altar was foreign and even dangerous.

The altar was a place of regular sacrifice and people would often build these altars either at the direction of God or after a great victory. The whole idea, made clear in scripture, was that the people were required to make constant sacrifices at these altars to ensure God heard them. When we carry this idea forward into the New Testament church, there is an underlying sentiment that is often reinforced because of what the altar meant in the Old Testament.

What I have often witnessed in many churches are people I refer to as "altar runners." Unfortunately, our churches have actually encouraged people to become these altar runners. At the end of service, in some churches, there is what is referred to as an altar call. This is a time when people are encouraged to come forward to the altar and lay down their burdens or sins at the feet of God. I've often seen many preachers keep preaching until these "altars" are full.

Unfortunately, I was among those altar runners. When the invitation was made to come down to the altar and pray, I often responded. What began to develop in my life was a pattern of going down to the altar during service to "cleanse" my conscience, then beating myself up during the week when I messed up. When we incorporate this idea of going to a certain place to confess those sins, we pull ourselves back to the old way of doing things.

God tells us that, as blood-bought believers, we carry God with us. There is no need for special places or special actions. This was how things were in the Old Testament assembly and, for those people; it was the right thing to do. When this idea is lived out in our lives, we can become people who live a compartmental life.

When the curtain was torn apart in Jerusalem that day and Jesus Christ proclaimed "It is finished," God no longer kept Himself in certain places. *Not only did the torn curtain signify we could approach God but now God comes to us.* God was on the move and we could access His presence at any time, in any place.

Search in the Old Testament and record how many times altars appear in the Old Testament. Now examine the New Testament and see how many times the word appears. The altar is referenced frequently in the Old Testament. However, instead of finding altars in the New Testament, we find a cross.

Consider the words of Jesus on the cross: "It is finished." There is finality in that statement that an altar doesn't represent. The altar allows us to constantly revisit those areas of our lives that need work. The cross shows us Jesus completed the work, not us.

Except for Revelation, a book of prophecy which many claim to understand, the altar is strangely absent in the New Testament.

Nowhere in the New Testament, after Jesus' crucifixion does the altar apply to us! In fact in the letter to the Hebrews the writer says just that:

> We have an altar, whereof they have no right to eat
> which serve the tabernacle. Hebrews 13:10 KJV

The writer of Hebrews knew the system of worship in those days. The altar held great meaning to those people, but possibly more meaning than we understand.

> Seven days thou shalt make an atonement for the altar, and sanctify it; and it shall be an altar most holy: whatsoever toucheth the altar shall be holy. Exodus 29:37 KJV

We often use the word serving to mean carrying out a duty or obligation. But that's not the entire picture painted here in Exodus. The people actually served the altar! Now the contradiction we see in our church services is made plain. How can we serve the altar and serve Jesus? We can't! *The altar is where Man served God; the cross is where God served man.* As long as we continually revisit that altar, we continue to try and make things right by the law. When we accept the grace of God at the cross, we move ourselves out of the way to allow God to do what only He can do: finally, set us free!

The New Testament letter to the Hebrews is rich with these descriptions of the finished work of Jesus Christ. All through this letter, the phrase "better than" is repeated over and over again. There is a distinction between the altar of sacrifice and the cross of Jesus. In fact, scriptures say Jesus was the altar. The Bible tells us the sins of the world were placed on Jesus to pay our sin debt once and for all. Jesus became our altar!

> For the Law, since it has only a shadow of the good things to come and not the very form of things, can never, by the same sacrifices which they offer continually year by year, make perfect those who draw near. Otherwise, would they not have ceased to be offered, because the worshipers, having once been cleansed, would no longer have had consciousness of sins? But in those sacrifices there is a reminder of sins year by year. For it is impossible for the blood

97

of bulls and goats to take away sins. Therefore, when He comes into the world, He says, "Sacrifice and offering You have not desired, But a body You have prepared for Me; In whole burnt offerings and sacrifices for sin You have taken no pleasure." Then I said, 'Behold, I have come (In the scroll of the book it is written After saying above, "Sacrifices and offerings and whole burnt offerings and sacrifices for sin You have not desired, nor have You taken pleasure in them" (which are offered according to the Law), then He said, "Behold, I have come to do Your will." He takes away the first in order to establish the second. By this will we have been sanctified through the offering of the body of Jesus Christ once for all. Every priest stands daily ministering and offering time after time the same sacrifices, which can never take away sins; but He, having offered one sacrifice for sins for all time, sat down at the right hand of God. Hebrews 10:1-12

The sacrifices placed on all of those altars could never be enough to accomplish what was needed for humanity. In fact, it required a constant revisiting of these offenses at an altar. But notice the finality of what was accomplished by Christ.

...but He, having offered one sacrifice for sins for all time, sat down at the right hand of God. Hebrews 10:12

I've often explained the difference between an altar and the cross when speaking to churches. Usually I meet with resistance because people have, for at least the past one hundred or so years, "found God" at these altars. I understand the symbolic representation of the altar and what it is has come to mean for so many people over the years. But the altar is no longer needed because of the cross.

I challenge you to research the meaning of the altar in The Old Testament and how it became a mainstay in our New Testament churches. What you find may surprise you.

I have no doubt that those who encourage people to go down to these altars in our churches, to make a decision for Christ, are godly women and men. My intent is not to challenge their spirituality, but to challenge traditions that can trap us. In scripture we find freedom in the cross we could never find at an altar. In fact, as we revisit Hebrews, the writer has something to say about those who insist on altars.

> We have an altar from which those who serve the tabernacle have no right to eat. Hebrews 13:10

The altar (found in the temple) limits us. There is a better, permanent life-altering symbol of freedom: the Cross of Jesus. The cross is a punctuation mark in history. It symbolizes for us, the dividing line in time when God was once found in a central temple for a few certain people, to a time after the cross where all have access to His grace.

Take that statement above from Hebrews at face value. The temple had special washings that were required in order to enter and special people who had special functions during the time of sacrifice at those altars. The altar was always meant to be a reminder of how badly humanity had messed up.

One of the most powerful examples of how far removed the idea of an altar should be is found in the first chapter of Acts. People from all over gathered to hear the very first sermon of Peter. Check the Bible and you'll find no mention of altars. But we do find the cross and at that cross we find 3,000 new believers ushered into the Kingdom of God with power and by grace.

While establishing his apostolic authority in Corinth, Paul said these words to the church:

> Do ye not know that they which minister about holy things live of the things of the temple? and they which wait at the altar are partakers with the altar? 1 Corinthians 9:13 KJV

Paul was using words with meaning to those in the church. And while Paul may have not meant to show the contrary action of the altar vs. the cross, it becomes plain to us. Those who serve at the altar receive what they get from that altar. If we rely on altars instead of a cross, we receive from that altar exactly what that altar has to offer.

To some, all this may sound like an argument of semantics. An altar or cross: what's the difference?

Jesus didn't pay the price for the world on an altar.

Jesus doesn't tell us to take up our altar and follow him.

Jesus didn't carry an altar to Golgotha.

The altar brings to mind all the things we messed up. As a result of these mess-ups, animals paid yearly the price for humanity. The animals were led to slaughter.

The altar wasn't a place of grace. It was a place where thousands of animals met their end. The cross is that place of grace because it was meant for us. God made the rules, He enforced the rules and He paid the price for inability to keep the rules He enforced. That's grace.

I encourage you to read through the Bible and see for yourself how the altar and cross stand at odds with each other after the crucifixion. What was once a place of failure and constant reminder of those failures has, at the cross, run its course. If we are constantly pulled to a place of remembering those fallings and failures, we can never fully embrace the *finished* work of Jesus. True grace changes everything.

Chapter 9

Which Jesus?

For this reason He is the mediator of a new covenant, so that, since a death has taken place for the redemption of the transgressions that were committed under the first covenant, those who have been called may receive the promise of the eternal inheritance. For where a covenant is, there must of necessity be the death of the one who made it. For a covenant is valid only when men are dead, for it is never in force while the one who made it lives. Hebrews 9:15-17

God's plan for humanity was unfolding before the eyes of the world. His plan for redemption was in the body of Jesus. Power and peace were present in the same person with just the right amount of each. As believers, we are amazed at the way Jesus stood His ground when the religious elite of that time challenged Him. Reading through the gospel accounts of His life has been a source of inspiration for many people, believers and non-believers alike. Many have tried to emulate His life, with limited success.

From numerous biblical sources we are often encouraged to live our lives much in the same way as Jesus. But think for a moment when and where Jesus lived His life. It was in a place that a foreign nation had conquered. It was a time when people were burdened by so many taxes and laws that they had all but given up hope.

As Jesus moved about, He healed and fed the people both physically and spiritually. He was often found acting in a way completely contrary to popular teaching of His day. In fact, this was what ultimately led to His death on the cross.

During the "seeking phase" of my walk with Christ, I tried over and over to walk the way He walked. I tried to do what He did and say what He said. On the outside, it all looked good. However, I was dying a slow death inside, and I couldn't invite someone to experience that. I couldn't share the Gospel news because it wasn't good news to me. I believed in hell and knew that I didn't want to end up there. But truthfully, I was in such turmoil from trying to live this life that would keep me from hell that I created a hell of sorts for myself which I lived every day. Something wasn't adding up. I read the words of Jesus and knew He was the answer, but what He was saying didn't manifest itself in my life, no matter how hard I tried.

This wasn't the life I wanted, nor was it the life Jesus promised:

> Come unto me, all ye that labour and are heavy laden, and I will give you rest. Take my yoke upon you, and learn of me; for I am meek and lowly in heart: and ye shall find rest unto your souls. For my yoke is easy, and my burden is light. Matthew 11:28-30 KJV

One day, while preparing for a sermon, I was studying the passages above and, like a lightning bolt, the realization dawned on me. *I was following the Jesus that walked the streets, not the Jesus who, by the power of God, stepped out of a borrowed tomb!*

This was the Jesus who walked, healed, prayed and ministered to all those who would come. But this Jesus had His limits. He left cities that wouldn't accept Him and did no miracles in those towns. He got tired and, at one point, came into contact with a woman that made "virtue go out from Him:"

> And Jesus, immediately knowing in himself that virtue
> had gone out of him, turned him about in the press,
> and said, who touched my clothes? Mark 5:30 KJV

For many of us who call Jesus Savior, we are much like the
disciples who followed Jesus during His earthly ministry. We are told
Jesus is our example and our lives should look like His. But there is a
problem with that approach: We can't! Even the disciples who were
with Him day in and day out couldn't live that life. Peter stumbled;
James and John were ready to call fire from heaven down on those
who wouldn't believe; Judas betrayed Him. To those of us who insist
on holding on to this Jesus, Jesus Himself speaks about the necessity
of His earthly departure:

> Nevertheless I tell you the truth; It is expedient for
> you that I go away: for if I go not away, the Comforter
> will not come unto you; but if I depart, I will send
> him unto you. John 16:7 KJV

What escaped me during my early years became apparent to me
as I read the Bible through this new set of lenses. Years of honest,
well-meaning Bible teachers that told me the New Testament began
with the Gospels, and this influenced my understanding of the New
Testament. What I discovered as I read deeper into the texts made
complete sense and reflected what other writers of the Bible had
clearly stated. *The New Testament didn't begin with the Gospels
of the New Testament; it began in the Gospels after Jesus was
resurrected:*

> For this reason He is the mediator of a new covenant,
> so that, since a death has taken place for the redemption
> of the transgressions that were committed under the
> first covenant, those who have been called may receive
> the promise of the eternal inheritance. For where a
> covenant is, there must of necessity be the death of the

one who made it. For a covenant is valid only when men are dead, *for it is never in force while the one who made it lives.* Hebrews 9:15-17 (italics mine)

Did you read that? A covenant is only valid when men are dead. The Gospels give us insight into a specific time during the *life* of Jesus. The Old Covenant was still in effect during His life. But when He gave His life for us, the New Covenant was put into effect, just as God planned.

Things began to make sense. Much of what Jesus taught came from the Old Testament law; after all, He was the expert. As this understanding settled upon me, what I read in the Bible not only began to make sense, it also revealed my need for Jesus. Not the earthly Son of God that had walked the streets of Jerusalem, but Jesus the Son of God who sits at God's right hand that has given me His power and His own inheritance.

With this new revelation, I began to read the Bible and about the life Jesus lived in a completely different way.

THE SERMON ON THE MOUNT

Many refer to the first part of the Sermon on the Mount as the Beatitudes. It was Jesus' first public sermon. There have been many sermons preached on this particular passage of scripture. I have seen numerous pictures depicting Jesus sitting on a hill with hundreds of people surrounding him. Jesus is usually pictured sitting on a rock, on the side of a hill speaking to the multitudes. No doubt there may have been some people coming and going during His sermon, but the intended audience that day was His disciples. Both Matthew and Luke record that Jesus called His disciples to Him, and then He began to teach

When Jesus saw the crowds, He went up on the mountain; and after He sat down, *His disciples came to Him.* He opened His mouth and began to teach them, saying, Matthew 5:1-2 (italics mine)

> *And turning His gaze toward His disciples,* He began to say, "Blessed are you who are poor, for yours is the kingdom of God. Luke 6:20 (italics mine)

For the longest time, I had pictured Jesus and saw motion pictures depicting Him speaking to the multitudes. However, He wasn't. He spoke directly to the disciples. Those men were Jewish and had been raised in Jewish homes, schooled in the synagogues, been involved in temple worship and memorized the Torah as young men.

The very first words from His mouth were:

> Blessed are the poor in spirit: for theirs is the kingdom of heaven. Matthew 5:3 KJV

To fully understand the words Jesus spoke that day requires us to fully understand the meaning of the words poor in spirit. The word "poor" comes from the word pauper, someone who is broke, bankrupt, destitute and unable to pay their bills. Jesus was pointing to the debt humanity had with God. Then He continues and tells the disciples "theirs is the kingdom of God." Just those words alone point to God's grace. To enter the kingdom of God requires recognition in our own lives of the lack of ability to do any of the things Jesus taught on our own. Have you ever tried to be "poor in spirit?"

As we continue to read further, we begin to see how Jesus is taking conventional knowledge of the law and, rather than holding people to the letter of the law, he addresses the spirit of the law. In other words, he addresses the reason the law is even in place:

> For I say unto you, That except your righteousness shall exceed the righteousness of the scribes and Pharisees, ye shall in no case enter into the kingdom of heaven. Matthew 5:20 KJV

The Pharisees were the religious elite of that day. They kept the law and added laws to the law so as not to even come close to breaking the original law. How many of us do the same? We enter the Gospels and set up lists of things we will and won't do, things we do and don't do, based on these teachings of Jesus, without fully understanding the motivation behind Jesus' Sermon on the Mount. He was showing us the futility of trying to do things ourselves. He was pointing to God's grace all along.

Take the next few passages of Matthew Chapter 5. Six times Jesus states "you have heard it said" or a variation of that statement, and then He follows this by saying "But I say unto you." Read Matthew 5:21-24:

> Ye have heard that it was said by them of old time, Thou shalt not kill; and whosoever shall kill shall be in danger of the judgment: But I say unto you, That whosoever is angry with his brother without a cause shall be in danger of the judgment: and whosoever shall say to his brother, Raca, shall be in danger of the council: but whosoever shall say, Thou fool, shall be in danger of hell fire. Therefore if thou bring thy gift to the altar, and there rememberest that thy brother hath ought against thee; Leave there thy gift before the altar, and go thy way; first be reconciled to thy brother, and then come and offer thy gift. Matthew 5:21-24 KJV

If we still operated by those standards and with the altar in place, who would actually be able to offer anything at all? Remember, Jesus isn't just saying we should forgive someone who has wronged us; He is saying to reconcile with someone we have wronged! How many times have we cut someone off or said a cross word to someone at a checkout counter during rush hour? According to the laws and teachings of that time, before we could offer any sacrifice at all, there would have to be reconciliation. If we were still under the law, the very act of approaching the altar in our churches still having "ought" with someone, would mean we are doing exactly the opposite of what Christ said to do. Talk about confusion!

COMMUNION

Many take what Paul says in his letter to the church at Corinth about the act of participating in communion, and mingle sacrificial law with a grace-filled act of love. We use the Old Testament understanding of the altar as we approach the communion table. The act of communion has nothing to do with what we have done. It's about what Jesus has already done, and we are told to remember this act.

Apparently, at that church in Corinth, there were those who were observing the Lord's Supper in their actions, but had missed the depth of what they were doing in their hearts. There were those who were getting drunk on the wine and there were those who were eating too much and shorting those who had little.

To these people Paul says:

> Wherefore whosoever shall eat this bread, and drink this cup of the Lord, unworthily, shall be guilty of the body and blood of the Lord. But let a man examine himself, and so let him eat of that bread, and drink of that cup. 1 Corinthians 11:27-28 KJV

Many take the words we read in verse 28 and apply the law to an act of grace. However, the communion table is not an altar; it is a table of fellowship. In fact, the word communion is the same word for fellowship. When we take the elements of communion unworthily, Paul is not referring to any sin in our lives; he is referring to our relationship with Jesus and that relationship alone makes us worthy to take communion.

I can't count the times I have witnessed those believers who have sat in their chairs refusing to take communion because they have an "ought" against someone. Without fail, their response is, "There is something in my life I have to get right before I take communion." The Old Testament way of sacrifice and the New Testament act of communion are mingled:

> Leave there thy gift before the altar, and go thy way; first be reconciled to thy brother, and then come and offer thy gift. Matthew 5:24 KJV

> But let a man examine himself, and so let him eat of that bread, and drink of that cup. 1 Corinthians 11:28 KJV

I admit there are times when I have taken those elements during that sacred time after having cross words with someone earlier in the day or week. But what I have experienced is grace from God in the realization of what He has done, and my response is always to right that wrong. When I come to that communion table and take those elements because of who He is instead of what I have done, right or wrong, I am ready to be filled with His compassion and love that motivates my actions.

The statement Jesus made to His disciple about righting a wrong before offering a sacrifice on the altar was made by the Jesus who lived under the law. He had to live under this law in order to fulfill that law. The Jesus who told us to "take the bread and wine in remembrance of me" was that sacrifice *and* the altar. When Jesus became that sacrifice, He fulfilled all the requirements of the law in full.

Now, when we take communion, we are participants in His actions here on earth because of His invitation and completed work, not because of what we do or don't do.

The Church, in its eagerness to properly represent the solemnness of communion, has overstepped its bounds.

In my first pastorate, I was not allowed to serve communion because I was not ordained. By their standards, no person could serve these elements unless they were properly recognized by the denomination. So for about seven months, I pastored this church and, when we had our time of communion each month, I had to contact a neighboring church to request the services of an ordained deacon to perform this act for me. That never did sit right in my spirit. So I did what we all should when confronted by a question: I went to the Bible. Guess what? There were no ordination standards given, nor were there specially appointed people to serve the communion elements.

At the church where I serve, we take the act of communion seriously. So seriously in fact, that we ask others who usually only partake of communion to actually lead us in communion. No ordination required. What I have discovered from talking to those people who are given this opportunity is just how deep into scripture they went to understand communion. Their relationship with God was strengthened and their place in the kingdom was shown to them. We are all one in the same, with different functions, but with the same Spirit. This simple act of asking someone to lead the church in something they have witnessed for years took them to a deeper walk with Jesus. They began to understand the grace of God in Jesus. They read about how, even though Jesus knew His disciples would betray and leave Him, He stayed the course for us. Instead of merely hearing about the grace of God, they experienced that grace. When we mix the old way of doing things, where only the chosen were allowed to participate, with the new way, where all believers are equal in spiritual status, we do the kingdom a huge disservice and slam the door of grace in the face of those who need to know this grace.

Some of the most compelling passages found in the Bible that show us the danger of mixing the old and new way are in three of the four Gospel accounts:

> No man putteth a piece of new cloth unto an old garment, for that which is put in to fill it up taketh from the garment, and the rent is made worse. Neither do men put new wine into old bottles: else the bottles

break, and the wine runneth out, and the bottles perish: but they put new wine into new bottles, and both are preserved. Matthew 9:16–17 KJV

No man also seweth a piece of new cloth on an old garment: else the new piece that filled it up taketh away from the old, and the rent is made worse. And no man putteth new wine into old bottles: else the new wine doth burst the bottles, and the wine is spilled, and the bottles will be marred: but new wine must be put into new bottles. Mark 2:21–22 KJV

And he spake also a parable unto them; No man putteth a piece of a new garment upon an old; if otherwise, then both the new maketh a rent, and the piece that was taken out of the new agreeth not with the old. And no man putteth new wine into old bottles; else the new wine will burst the bottles, and be spilled, and the bottles shall perish. But new wine must be put into new bottles; and both are preserved. No man also having drunk old wine straightway desireth new: for he saith, the old is better. Luke 5:36–39 KJV

Notice the comparisons: new cloth on an old piece of clothing and new wine in old wine skins. These examples may be slightly foreign to us, depending on our background, but from experience I can tell you about having new cloth on old garments. As a boy, the knees of my pants took a lot of abuse. My family didn't have a lot of money, so patches were put on the holes that I would inevitably wear in my pants. But those repairs weren't a permanent solution. In fact, I was lucky if I made it to the end of the year. The old pants would tear away from the new patch and, by the end of the year, they were only fit to use as rags.

Wine, in the time of Jesus was kept in "skins." These skins were usually made from the stomach of a goat. As long as the wine placed in the skins had already undergone the fermentation process, there was no problem. But putting new wine in these skins was a recipe for disaster because of the violence of the fermentation process. This process would give off gasses that would swell the skins to their breaking point until they wouldn't hold the wine.

This is an accurate depiction of how, as believers, we take what was given to us under the old covenant and try to mate this old way with the new way of grace Jesus gives. It won't work. *When we have special people doing special things for God, it places us back under the old covenant.*

The new wine refers to the new covenant which has to be placed in new "wineskins" that will take all the pressure applied to it. But the most telling picture of what most of the church experiences is found in Luke:

> No man also having drunk old wine straightway desireth
> new: for he saith, The old is better. Luke 5:39 KJV

The Jewish people of that day had, for years, been under the law. Even though the burden was heavy, they knew what to expect. Law is predictable, but grace isn't. We live our lives in a system that says if you do A, then B will follow. As believers, this is often how we approach our relationship with God. If I go to church, I will be blessed. If I give, I will be blessed. It's all based on our action and not on the completed work of Jesus Christ. This approach sounds good and may even produce some limited results. This is because of a principle God has already put into place:

> Be not deceived; God is not mocked: for whatsoever a
> man soweth, that shall he also reap. Galatians 6:7 KJV

The promise Jesus makes us goes far beyond that principle of sowing and reaping. It promises blessing in spiritual places, things not of this world. When we pull ourselves back under those ways, we get what we ask for and that's it. God's grace in Jesus gives us more than we could ever dream. But for some, the old way is better. It's more predictable. It doesn't take faith to live out the law of sowing and reaping.

Jesus is giving those people that day a glimpse of what was to come, something we have access to right now. We don't have to wait until we get to heaven to be blessed. That's the grace that changes everything.

Chapter 10

Under Pressure

And no man putteth new wine into old bottles; else the new wine will burst the bottles, and be spilled, and the bottles shall perish. Luke 5:37

Unfortunately, I have seen this "bursting" in the lives of many people in our churches today. It comes from the pressure we put upon ourselves or pressure that others put on us as we try to "live up to" God's standards. Understand this: if we can't do enough to get ourselves out of the mess we are in to begin with, we won't be able to do enough after we meet Jesus. It is not, and never has been, about how clean our outside looks and how well we function or about the good things we do or produce. It is what Jesus produces in us.

Secrets from the Vine

I am the true vine, and my Father is the husbandman. Every branch in me that beareth not fruit he taketh away: and every branch that beareth fruit, he purgeth it, that it may bring forth more fruit. Now ye are clean through the word which I have spoken unto you. Abide in me, and I in you. As the branch cannot bear fruit of itself, except it abide in the vine; no more

113

can ye, except ye abide in me. I am the vine, ye are the branches: He that abideth in me, and I in him, the same bringeth forth much fruit: for without me ye can do nothing. If a man abide not in me, he is cast forth as a branch, and is withered; and men gather them, and cast them into the fi re, and they are burned. If ye abide in me, and my words abide in you, ye shall ask what ye will, and it shall be done unto you. Herein is my Father glorified, that ye bear much fruit; so shall ye be my disciples. John 15:1-8 KJV

In titling this section, I choose to use the word secret not because what Jesus tells us in John is a secret, but because our lack of biblical understanding and sound teaching on this passage has kept these truths secret.

There are many components in the previous passage that all work together to produce the effect God wants to see in our lives. First is the husbandman, who is the Father and tends the garden. Second is the vine, which is Jesus. Third, the branches that bear the fruit, that's us. Fourth is the fruit.

I have spent many a Sunday morning listening to a sermon about how the life of a believer should have fruit as witness to what God has done in our lives. Then subtlety, the focus is turned on how I'm not living a godly enough life to produce this fruit. This is a case of the tail wagging the dog.

Somehow, through all these years of preaching and teaching, the focus has remained on how our efforts produce these Godly fruits. If I love enough, give enough, serve enough, then the fruit comes. But guess what? It never did for me, and I'll venture to guess, it has not for many who may be reading this book. It seems that the way to God is through our own effort when that passage is explained in many churches today. Does any of that sound like old wine?

When I have the time, I like to relax in front of the television set. One evening, I was flipping through the channels when I came upon a televised church service where an elderly pastor was preaching on John 15. Curious as to how he would approach this particular passage, I laid down the remote control and listened. He had on stage with him a branch planted in a pot of dirt. After reading this passage, his message was simple, but profound.

Jesus does the work in our lives that produces this fruit.

The word for "bear" means we are fruit holders, not producers. Finally! Someone was "rightly dividing the word of God". To this day, I wish that I could remember his name to give that pastor the credit for this example, which I have used in my own church to explain this often misquoted and misunderstood passage.

As he spoke, he talked about how we as people run ahead of God and try to do all these good things, which require a huge amount of effort on our part. At this point in the sermon, he contorted his face in exaggerated agony, and after a few seconds, stuck a grape on the end of one of those bare branches planted in that pot of soil. He exclaimed "That's what it looks like when we do the work Jesus is supposed to do in us!" Sound familiar?

When Jesus tells us to abide in Him and we will bear much fruit, He is speaking about the close relationship we have with Him. From that relationship and from His power, that fruit is produced. Then, we carry that fruit. The pressure to produce is lifted from our shoulders and placed on Jesus, who always follows through with what He promises. The only thing secretive about this passage is the realization that, *as believers, we don't have to try to abide in Him; God has already put us there.* This is what the phrase, "in Christ," means!

> Paul, an apostle of Jesus Christ by the will of God, to the saints which are at Ephesus, and to the faithful in Christ Jesus. Ephesians 1:1KJV

> Being justified freely by his grace through the redemption that is in Christ Jesus. Romans 3:24KJV

So we, being many, are one body in Christ, and every one members one of another. Romans 12:5KJV

But by His doing you are in Christ Jesus, who became to us wisdom from God, and righteousness and sanctification, and redemption. 1 Corinthians 1:30

Unto the church of God which is at Corinth, to them that are sanctified in Christ Jesus, called to be saints, with all that in every place call upon the name of Jesus Christ our Lord, both theirs and ours. 1 Corinthians 1:2 KJV

Abiding in Christ simply means, staying where God has already put us.

Nowhere in Scripture does Paul or any of the New Testament authors imply we have to work on abiding in Him. So why do we struggle with something we already have? Simply stated, we are conditioned this way.

We live in a world of deadlines and time constraints. It's no wonder many of us incorporate this idea of production into our lives with God. We have been programed that way. The world reinforces this idea on a daily, sometimes hourly, basis. We punch time clocks and are paid for what we produce. Our livelihoods depend on our production. If we don't produce, we will probably lose our jobs, homes and many other things our jobs fund. But the gospel is not, and never has been, about that kind of pressure. In fact, it's just the opposite.

Not long after contacting the publisher to begin the process of publishing this book, I felt the pressure mounting.

"What if I couldn't finish the book? What if my writings skills were not up to par and made no sense? What if I ran out of things to say? What would people I knew say about this book? What if people I had known before Christ tried to discredit me because they "knew" me and some of the things I had done?"

When these thoughts came into my mind, I tried to ignore them, but the tapes kept playing over and in over my head. "I'm not smart enough; I haven't even been to college. Well-known people in Christian circles endorse most of the books I read. Who am I?"

But that reassurance that God promises answered all these questions. As it says in the Bible, *He that abideth in me, and I in him, the same bringeth forth much fruit.*

That's the Grace that changes everything.

YOU MUST BE YOKING ME!

> Take my yoke upon you, and learn of me; for I am meek and lowly in heart: and ye shall find rest unto your souls. For my yoke is easy, and my burden is light. Matthew 11:29-30 KJV

I couldn't resist the play on words! While it may not be the outward response of those who read these profound words of Jesus and His promise to us, inwardly, as we try to live "the good life," our spirits become burdened with the knowledge of our shortcomings. This yoke Jesus describes doesn't seem as easy and light as He says. So what do we do? Try harder. How's that working for us? I can't speak for anyone else, but as for me, I gave up!

The yoke Jesus refers to was often used on farms to yoke oxen together as they plowed the fields. Many times, farmers would put a younger ox together with an older ox to train it. The older ox had more experienced and would "break in" the younger ox, which allowed the farmer to get more work done in a shorter amount of time. But this example falls far short of what Jesus was referring to and probably had some in the crowd scratching their head. The reason? Both oxen pulled the plow, and even if the older oxen pulled more, there was still work involved for both oxen.

Many will look at this and ask, "But what about when Jesus said, 'Take up your cross and follow me?' Isn't that basically the same

117

thing?" Possibly, if Jesus hadn't of made the flowing statement prior to encouraging others to take His yoke:

> Come unto me, all ye that labor and are heavy laden,
> and I will give you rest. Matthew 11:28 KJV

So let me get this straight: when we are tired and burdened, He wants us to take His yoke and somehow this is rest? Sounds like more work to me. Even if I am yoked with Jesus, there is still work happening and I still have to pull my weight. That doesn't sound like rest to me.

Let's put ourselves back in those days when Jesus ministered. Remember, Jesus was in a culture and a place far removed from American farming. No machinery, no electricity, no combustion engine to power plows or any other farming implement. Even with the modern technology of today, farming is still hard work. Our confusion stems from our misunderstanding of the term "yoke".

Jesus was actually referring to the teachings many had been sitting under with other spiritual mentors. The word yoke in those days also meant "teaching." If you sat under a teacher, you took his yoke. In short, Jesus was saying, "Take my teaching on and follow me. What you'll find is a God who wants a relationship with you and has made that possible." Jesus never worked for God; God worked through Him in everything. Jesus wants the same for us. His strength and power flowed from the Father. He did nothing in His own strength, but in the strength and power of God. That's His plan for us.

This understanding lifted years of burdens from my shoulders. I began to understand that Jesus wants me to join Him in a mission that He is already on. He is blazing the trail; I'm just following. Aside from the pressures of everyday life, when we take these pressures into the church we burden people just like the Pharisees did in those days when Jesus confronted them.

The word tribulation in the Bible means pressure. Tribulation is always referred to in the Bible as those things we face outside of the church. It's the world Satan controls, working against us. Unfortunately, what many experience in the church is tribulation, not freedom. Sadly, many sit in church while rules and regulations are piled higher and higher on their shoulders. The pressure mounts, and many decide it's just not worth it and walk away. Many decide there is no hope for them and that the gospel isn't for them, and never was, because they'll never be that good.

In those days, Jesus met many who had the same thought. The Romans that conquered their city placed an oppressive burden on them with heavy taxes. To make matters worse, their own leaders were making things unbearable. This is not far from what I see in our churches today, where defeated Christians live like spiritual paupers who have the keys to the kingdom in their hand, only to have some spiritual expert snatch them away. We need grace.

On any given Sunday there may be someone sitting beside us who has been beaten up by life. They have bought into the lie of the enemy that tells them; the way life is now, is how it will always be. When these people turn to the church for answers; what answer will they receive?

Long before I went back to church, my wife attended a church service she would never forget. She shared this experience with me later and, quite frankly, I couldn't blame her for not going back. The service started normal enough, but as the pastor continued to speak, people jumped up and started running up and down the aisles speaking words my wife had never heard. It scared her to death and she never went back. The sad thing was my wife was looking for answers. Our relationship was on the rocks and things didn't look too promising for us. She had received Jesus in the front seat of her car on the way to work one morning, and she was diligently looking.

Jason, one of our pastors on staff, shared his first church experience with me. While things weren't as extreme for him, the outcome was the same. He had received Christ and was digging into the Bible for days on end. He was looking for God and how God would move in his life. So he took the next logical step; he went to church. What he experienced was like a funeral. There was no life, no joy, nothing that would make him want anything to do with God. He is thankful he had that relationship with God before going to that church. What would others tell us if asked about their church experiences?

What I have come to understand in a deep way is that what people are looking for is truth. People aren't looking for a show, and they're not looking for more rules. They are looking for hope. God's grace is that hope. In His grace there is everything we will ever need to live in this life and the life to come. That's the grace that changes everything.

Chapter 11

Just Getting By

Blessed be the God and Father of our Lord Jesus
Christ, who hath blessed us with all spiritual blessings
in heavenly places in Christ. Ephesians 1:3 KJV

When we begin to understand our place in the Kingdom of God and what blessings are already ours because of our position in the Kingdom, we won't be satisfied with second best. The church has settled for second best long enough and has just been "getting by" for too many years. When we rightly understand that salvation not only means we spend an eternity with God after this life, but that in this life we have a God who has blessed us, our whole outlook will change.

Many Americans live paycheck to paycheck. All our financial experts say that our economy is in the tank and things will only get worse. However, we haven't experienced this in my house. While ministry doesn't always pay well, my family has never missed a meal, nor have we ever missed a house payment, car payment or been late on any other bill. There are some things we would like to do, but financially it would be ill-advised not because of the economy, but because of our mission here on earth.

> For he that soweth to his flesh shall of the flesh reap
> corruption; but he that soweth to the Spirit shall of
> the Spirit reap life everlasting. Galatians 6:8 KJV

There was a time in my life when I did miss payments and had to scrape money together to make ends meet. But during that time, I was living a life solely focused on getting by. God intends and provides a way for His people to not just make it, but to overcome. But none of this happens if we constantly settle for second best.

In God's economy, finances are a low priority. In fact, if you try to coerce God into blessing you financially, you have pulled yourself back under the Old Covenant where we are working for God's blessings rather than working from God's blessings.

Unfortunately, much like our financial life, our spiritual life is also a paycheck to paycheck meeting with God. We go to church and "meet" God there once a week, then for the other six days we struggle in our relationship with Him. God's intent towards us is not like a game of hide-and-seek where we visit with Him once a week, then are left to search for Him the rest of the time. This well-worn path is an invitation for the enemy to "trip us up:"

> Be sober, be vigilant; because your adversary the
> devil, as a roaring lion, walketh about, seeking whom
> he may devour. 1Peter 5:8 KJV

Lions are a predatory species. They often lie in wait for their prey in places they frequent, such as watering holes and particular travel routes. Think for a moment what places you frequent, whether that place is a thought you have or a place you go. With what addictions or bad thoughts do you struggle? When these thoughts happen, do you entertain those thoughts or do you turn those over to God? Much of what we blame on the devil, while it may have initiated with him, continues in our lives because of those well-worn paths we travel.

> But every man is tempted, when he is drawn away
> of his own lust, and enticed. Then when lust hath
> conceived, it bringeth forth sin: and sin, when it is
> finished, bringeth forth death. James 1:14-15 KJV

God's plan for us was never to just get by, but to overcome.

> As it is written, For thy sake we are killed all the day
> long; we are accounted as sheep for the slaughter.
> Nay, in all these things we are more than conquerors
> through him that loved us. Romans 8:36-37 KJV

The best example of defeating the devil happened in the wilderness prior to Jesus' ministry. Remember, we are told the Spirit led Jesus to this place to be tempted. Jesus showed us the power of God when the word of God is believed to be just that: the word from God to us!

We don't have a record of Jesus' life before His earthly ministry began, but it is safe to say that He spent many hours alone in the wilderness in communion with God prior to "going public." This may have been that well-worn path the enemy knew about. The Holy Spirit knew the enemy would be there in the wilderness. In fact the gospels record, the Holy Spirit led Jesus into the wilderness *to be tempted*. But read how Jesus won that battle and how to attain those victories:

> Then was Jesus led up of the Spirit into the wilderness
> to be tempted of the devil. And when he had fasted
> forty days and forty nights, he was afterward an
> hungered. And when the tempter came to him, he
> said, If thou be the Son of God, command that these
> stones be made bread. But he answered and said, It
> is written, Man shall not live by bread alone, but by
> every word that proceedeth out of the mouth of God.
> Then the devil taketh him up into the holy city, and
> setteth him on a pinnacle of the temple, And saith

unto him, If thou be the Son of God, cast thyself down: for it is written, He shall give his angels charge concerning thee: and in their hands they shall bear thee up, lest at any time thou dash thy foot against a stone. Jesus said unto him, It is written again, Thou shalt not tempt the Lord thy God. Again, the devil taketh him up into an exceeding high mountain, and sheweth him all the kingdoms of the world, and the glory of them; And saith unto him, All these things will I give thee, if thou wilt fall down and worship me. Then saith Jesus unto him, Get thee hence, Satan: for it is written, Thou shalt worship the Lord thy God, and him only shalt thou serve. Then the devil leaveth him, and, behold, angels came and ministered unto him. Matthew 4:1-11 KJV

We've probably all read about how Jesus defeated the devil by quoting scripture, but it's not just in His quoting of scripture that He gained the victory. He believed it! Jesus knew every word that came out of God's heart which the prophets recorded in the scriptures, were for Him. *When we actually believe God is talking directly to us, His power in our lives is unmistakable.* Such is the power, action, and blessing of grace to a believer.

For us, God not only makes these promises, but by Jesus' example proves that those promises are real. A quick review of scripture after Jesus' encounter with the enemy in the wilderness shows how many times Jesus returned to the wilderness.

And when he had sent the multitudes away, he went up into a mountain apart to pray: and when the evening was come, he was there alone. Matthew 14:23 KJV And he withdrew himself into the wilderness, and prayed. Luke 5:16 KJV

> When Jesus therefore perceived that they would
> come and take him by force, to make him a king,
> he departed again into a mountain himself alone.
> John 6:15 KJV

Consider for a moment that in a place where the greatest potential for defeat existed, came victory. But the enemy wasn't finished. In the Garden of Gethsemane, when Jesus faced His greatest battle, the potential for defeat existed, and Jesus worked from a place of victory. He defeated the enemy once and for all. Jesus never settled for second best and neither should we, but we often do. Consider these words found in Galatians:

> Be not deceived; God is not mocked: for whatsoever
> a man soweth, that shall he also reap. For he that
> soweth to his flesh shall of the flesh reap corruption;
> but he that soweth to the Spirit shall of the Spirit reap
> life everlasting. Galatians 6:7-8 KJV

When we read these words of Paul, what we fail to do is look at what God says *in its entirety*. For man to function in the world, God had two options. 1) Ignore the offense, which is impossible because of His perfect nature or 2) put certain laws in place to allow humanity to at least live in this fallen state. Before any of the laws were ever "on the books," God set into motion a way for humanity to live:

> And unto Adam he said, Because thou hast hearkened
> unto the voice of thy wife, and hast eaten of the tree,
> of which I commanded thee, saying, Thou shalt not
> eat of it: cursed is the ground for thy sake; in sorrow
> shalt thou eat of it all the days of thy life; Thorns also
> and thistles shall it bring forth to thee; and thou shalt
> eat the herb of the field; In the sweat of thy face shalt

thou eat bread, till thou return unto the ground; for out of it wast thou taken: for dust thou art, and unto dust shalt thou return. Genesis 3:17-19 KJV

While God cursed the ground, He didn't make it impossible to live in the world. However, man would have to claw his existence from the earth; he would have to work for it. This same "work for it" attitude permeates our existence today, and only the grace of God can reverse the curse.

The law of sowing and reaping ensures man can make it. In other words, we can get by. For those who choose this path apart from God, this law effectually ensures these people can at least make it in this world. Ever wonder why those who live a life of excess and debauchery never seem to get what we think they have coming? That's the law of sowing and reaping; what you plant, you'll pick. Work hard and you'll get returns.

Nevertheless, Paul tells us that whatever we produce is doomed for destruction, and that's not just a spiritual expression. Have you ever been to the funeral of a wealthy person? The service may be magnificent, but unless this person is known by God, that's as far as things go. Whatever accolades or possessions they have no longer matter.

Become religious and the law of sowing and reaping is still in effect. If our motivation isn't founded on the grace of Jesus, nothing we do in the name of religion will "get God's attention." Whatever it is you work for will usually come about, but God gives those who choose to follow Him and live in grace, more than they could ever imagine.

WHO ARE WE?

Nay, in all these things we are more than conquerors through him that loved us. Romans 8:37 KJV

Notice the word Paul uses to describe the children of God: conquerors. This word brings with it the idea of total and complete victory. Has that been your experience? According to the Bible, God never changes and never will. So if we agree that God doesn't change and He is incapable of lying, then the problem lies with us. Our identities are so wrapped up in what we do that in order for us to realize who we are, apart from what we do, we have listen to what our Creator says about us.

> And be not conformed to this world: but be ye transformed by the renewing of your mind, that ye may prove what is that good, and acceptable, and perfect, will of God. Romans 12:2 KJV

Let these words from God settle your spirit. Make copies and plaster them around your house. Copy them on sticky notes and put them in your cubicle at work. Write them in the front of your Bible. But most important of all, accept these words as promises from God to you.

> Know ye not that ye are the temple of God, and that the Spirit of God dwelleth in you? 1 Corinthians 3:16 KJV

We are often beaten over the head with this verse when we make mistakes. However, God's intention isn't for us to recoil in horror, but to understand that God's presence, His grace, is with us always:

> I am the vine, ye are the branches: He that abideth in me, and I in him, the same bringeth forth much fruit: for without me ye can do nothing. John 15:5 KJV

The pressure to perform is lifted off our shoulders. Christ lives in us and through us; we are already in Christ and there's no need for us to work to abide in Him. He produces, by His grace, those things that bring God glory and enable us to meet any circumstance we may face head-on.

> There is therefore now no condemnation to them
> which are in Christ Jesus. Romans 8:1 KJV

No matter how many times we fail, there is always grace available to us. Any condemnation we shoulder doesn't come from God, but from the enemy. God gives us the opportunity to repent or change direction; forgiveness has already been given at the cross.

> We know that whosoever is born of God sinneth not;
> but he that is begotten of God keepeth himself, and
> that wicked one toucheth him not. 1 John 5:18 KJV

Rather than viewing this passage as a standard we judge ourselves by, as the enemy would have us do, know this; God's view of us isn't as sinners, but as His children. *We have done what is required to "keep ourselves," which is trusting in God's grace through Jesus Christ and Him alone.* This ensures we are out of the enemy's reach:

> For God hath not given us the spirit of fear; but of power,
> and of love, and of a sound mind. 2 Timothy 1:7 KJV

As believers and citizens of the kingdom, we don't live in fear of the King. Any fear we may experience comes from the enemy. God isn't mad at us when we disappoint Him; He doesn't approve, but He corrects for our benefit, not His satisfaction:

> Who hath delivered us from the power of darkness,
> and hath translated us into the kingdom of his dear
> Son. Colossians 1:13 KJV

> In whom we have redemption through his blood,
> even the forgiveness of sins. Colossians 1:14 KJV

Our place of residency has changed. We now live in His righteousness, through His grace and power, because we have been totally forgiven!

> Henceforth I call you not servants; for the servant knoweth not what his lord doeth: but I have called you friends; for all things that I have heard of my Father I have made known unto you. John 15:15 KJV

Does it change the view you have of God when Jesus says He is your friend? We are not pawns in a cosmic chess game. Friends are those who care for us and what happens in our life. Think of how many times friends have come to our rescue. That's our relationship with God.

When I begin to realize how God looks at me, I begin to view myself differently. Often, our view of God is based on how we view ourselves. If God loves and treasures me, from that vantage point, my life with God begins to take on a completely different dimension. If I am convinced that I will never get things right and God's view of me changes, how can I ever feel safe enough to ever approach God? How can I go to God with anything if God is always mad at me because of my sin?

> Let us therefore come boldly unto the throne of grace that we may obtain mercy, and find grace to help in time of need. Hebrews 4:16 KJV

This passage in Hebrews gives hope to those who choose to embrace the Gospel of grace from God in Jesus Christ. Because of Jesus' intercession for us, God's grace is extended to us. The boldness we have is only possible if we accept this grace. Otherwise, we find ourselves groveling at the foot of the throne rather than boldly entering into the presence of God who wants to have a relationship with us. Grace changes everything!

Chapter 12

Making God in Our Image

> And God said, Let us make man in our image, after
> our likeness. Genesis 1:26

From the very beginning, we learn in the Bible that God formed man from the ground and breathed into his nostrils to give man life. From God we received our identities and our purpose. After the fall, as our relationship with God deteriorated, so did our understanding of Him. To explain the ways and actions of a God, who is Spirit (not *a* spirit, but Spirit), must have been a huge undertaking for those early prophets and teachers. But with the Spirit of God leading them and prompting their words, we have an extremely accurate description of God's nature.

But lack of study and scriptural understanding has often misrepresented God and His attributes. Have you ever noticed that people who struggle in their relationship with God often worship a God that has many of their same characteristics? People who follow all the rules understand God to be a taskmaster. Those who live life by the seat of their pants portray God as a whimsical spirit we can't fully know. Instead of us being made into the image of God, we remake God in our image.

GOD'S ANGER

And to wait for his Son from heaven, whom he raised from the dead, even Jesus, which delivered us from the wrath to come. 1 Timothy 1:10 KJV

For the wrath of God is revealed from heaven against all ungodliness and unrighteousness of men, who hold the truth in unrighteousness. Romans 1:18 KJV

For which things' sake the wrath of God cometh on the children of disobedience. Colossians 3:6 KJV

In the which ye also walked some time, when ye lived in them. Colossians 3:7 KJV

For God hath not appointed us to wrath, but to obtain salvation by our Lord Jesus Christ. 1Timothy 5:9 KJV

Much more then, being now justified by his blood, we shall be saved from wrath through him. Romans 5:9 KJV

A few years ago, during a visit with a close personal friend, the subject of God came up, as it usually does. As the conversation progressed, it became apparent that my friend's relationship with God was one based more in fear than in love. From the many other conversations I have had with believers over the years, I have found that many other believers share that same sentiment. In their minds, God gets mad when they don't live up to the standards found in the Bible, so they live in fear of God. From this theology, it is easy to understand why God would send earthquakes, tornadoes or tsunamis to make those people who crossed Him pay the price. Unfortunately, this couldn't be farther from the truth.

Read for a moment the passages at the beginning of this section. Do any of those passages imply that God is somehow mad at us and will send His wrath? From an Old Testament standpoint, these views are often accepted and even taught to many believers. But there is a flaw in this theology. While the flood was a worldwide event, God protected the righteous man Noah. Throughout the history of the nation of Israel, we find many "natural disasters." When these things occurred, the ones who paid the price were those who stood against God. I'm not saying that God hasn't, won't or couldn't cause a natural disaster on Earth; however, *Shouldn't we have a problem with a theology that would teach that God would think that collateral damage to His saints would be an acceptable option.* After all, many of our natural disasters claim believers and non-believers alike.

We apply the same concept in reverse when we say that God blesses us for living as a Christian nation. While it is true much of what we enjoy in the way of freedom comes from our Judeo-Christian roots, is it possible that we are claiming promises and blessings God made to the Israelites? Remember He was blessing and protecting the Jewish nation to ensure His plan of salvation came to fruition. When calamity came upon the Jewish nation it was because of their departure from God's will which endangered His plan. In fact those people were keeping many of the laws and probably appeared much more holy than we imagine. But God wanted their hearts not their hands.

> Sacrifice and offering thou didst not desire; mine ears hast thou opened: burnt offering and sin offering hast thou not required. Psalms 40:6 KJV

> For I desired mercy, and not sacrifice; and the knowledge of God more than burnt offerings. Hosea 6:6 KJV

I realize this may not be the most popular thought among many Christians, but grace is still grace. *Living as a nation following all His rules will never have the same effect on the world or each other, as living as people filled with His grace.*

The effect of humanity's abuse of our world has brought on many of these natural disasters often blamed on God's wrath. Over the last few hundred years, mankind has flexed his muscles against a power much greater than him. For thousands of years storms have ravaged places that were, until recently, largely unsettled. But because of the presence of people in these once uninhabited areas, these disasters harm, displace, and even kill people.

What about diseases? We have only to look at our lifestyles which account for many of these infirmities that afflict the human race. The reality is that humanity separated from God is capable of many heinous acts.

Three things happened at the Fall. We were separated from God, separated from others, and separated from creation. The outcome is what we see happening all around us. The reality we now live in is that humanity separated from God is capable of many wicked acts, both upon each other and our surroundings.

How many times have we heard the Bible verse "fear of the Lord is the beginning of wisdom?" While well-meaning saints are pointing our thinking in the right direction, living in the "fear of the Lord" is not how God desires His people to live. It is, as scripture clearly states, only *the beginning.* Fear is a great motivator, but sooner or later that fear will subside and complacency will set in. Think about how, as children, we followed our parent's rules until they were out of sight. Fear of the Lord starts what His grace finishes. To live in a fearful posture will never allow God's grace to permeate our beings and bring us into the wholeness He offers us.

Fear is an often misunderstood word and can distract us from His purposes in our life. Compare these two passages below:

> Nevertheless let every one of you in particular so love his wife even as himself; and the wife see that she reverence her husband. Ephesians 5:33 KJV

> And his mercy is on them that fear him from generation to generation. Luke 1:50 KJV

The word for fear and reverence used in both of these passages is the Greek word *phobos*. From this word is derived our English word phobia.

When Paul, in the book of Ephesians, encourages wives to show reverence to their husbands, it is the same word used when we find passages that tell us to "fear" God. But we should know if a marital relationship is based on fear, that relationship is destined for failure. No relationship between a husband and a wife will ever reach its full potential if that relationship is based on fear. The husband and wife may stay married, but the relationship will never grow into one of togetherness. It is the same in our relationship with God.

Paul uses the example of marriage to show us what our relationship with Christ should look like. Jesus is the groom; the body of believers, the bride. Christ loves us and we, in turn, from a position of those who have received His grace, revere (*phobos*) Him.

Many times, our view of God originates from dysfunctional relationships. Whether this relationship involves an angry spouse or parent, the actions of others we should have been able to trust, mar our image of God.

IS GOD HIDING?

Much of what is contained in the pages of this book is based on discussions I have had with others who profess faith in Jesus Christ. Many of these believers are godly people who sincerely desire to grow in their relationship with God. Unfortunately, much like the biblical scholars of Jesus' day, errant teaching has crept into the body of believers, rendering them ineffective as light bearers in a dark world. One the most damaging and unscriptural teaching about God and how He operates is the idea of a God who hides His face:

> LORD, why castest thou off my soul? why hidest thou thy face from me? Psalms 88:14 KJV

> Hide not thy face far from me; put not thy servant away in anger: thou hast been my help; leave me not, neither forsake me, O God of my salvation. Psalms 27:9 KJV

In the Psalms and other Old Testament books of the Bible, we often read the story of a person who has this sense that God is hiding from them. Usually this comes from an offense they have committed or some circumstance they find themselves in. From an Old Testament standpoint, this is an accurate depiction of what life in those days would have been like. But read on in the Bible as God unfolds His story and intersects humanity in the person of Jesus Christ:

> For I would not, brethren, that ye should be ignorant of this mystery, lest ye should be wise in your own conceits; that blindness in part is happened to Israel, until the fullness of the Gentiles be come in. Romans 11:25 KJV

> Having made known unto us the mystery of his will, according to his good pleasure which he hath purposed in himself: Ephesians 1:9 KJV

God's whole plan from the beginning was to present humanity with another option not available until He deemed it so.

> But when the fullness of the time was come, God sent forth his Son, made of a woman, made under the law,

> To redeem them that were under the law, that we might
> receive the adoption of sons. Galatians 4:4–5 KJV

What many in the Old Testament viewed as a hidden God was, in fact, a God unfolding His plan.

In the Wilderness?

A popular phrase I have heard from many is this "wilderness experience" they have with God. It's as if God has left them and their spiritual life is dry and uneventful, lacking the power He promises. Consider the story of Moses, which has been the source of much of this "wilderness thinking:"

> Now Moses kept the flock of Jethro his father in law,
> the priest of Midian: and he led the flock to the backside
> of the desert, and came to the mountain of God, even
> to Horeb. And the angel of the LORD appeared unto
> him in a flame of fire out of the midst of a bush: and
> he looked, and, behold, the bush burned with fire, and
> the bush was not consumed. Exodus 3:1–2 KJV

The Bible clearly states that Moses was in the wilderness. In fact, Moses was in the backside of the desert. That's quite a leap from just being in the wilderness. The backside of the desert is past the wilderness, take a right, and keep going until you see…nothing. This is a place where many believers often find themselves. Many believers are in a place where they say God isn't speaking to them, and they feel alone and vulnerable. But again in the light of scripture, this is a lie from the enemy whose sole purpose is to separate us from our life giving and grace filled source of peace.

Many cite the experience of the Israelites in the wilderness for those forty years to validate this wilderness theology. But remember those people were forced to live in the wilderness because of their lack of trust in God. God didn't turn His back on them; the Israelites turned their backs on God. *However, even in the wilderness God always spoke and took care of them.* The word wilderness even implies, in Hebrew, a place where God speaks and a place of communion with God.

Consider the amount of time Jesus spent in the wilderness. He often retired to the wilderness to spend time with God in prayer and communion. Being in the wilderness, when properly understood, is a place where God meets us, much like the burning bush that Moses encountered.

When I bowed my knee to Christ, this sense of a God who was strangely absent, dogged me for many years. But as God revealed to me in scripture who He really was, He also revealed to me I had begun to make God in the image of a person I barely knew, my father.

I have talked to many believers who carry the hurts from terrible childhoods and these hurts have hindered them in their walk with God. My childhood actually was good. My grandparents and my mom raised me with great love and tenderness. When I think back on my childhood, there were no terrible moments or family crises that I remember at an early age. I knew I was loved and never felt slighted by my father's absence. But as I matured, the absence of my father began to affect me in ways that were far from healthy. While I knew I was loved, I also knew that, on some level, I was unwanted. After all, isn't a father supposed to show love and affection and protect His children?

When I was around eight or nine years old, my Uncle Gene, one of the godliest men I know, led me down to the altar to receive Jesus. From that time on, I would read about a loving Heavenly Father who cared for me and wanted the best for me. Meanwhile, here on planet Earth, my earthly father never one time showed his face. From this understanding of fatherhood, my understanding of a Heavenly Father was formed. I began to make God into the image of a father that never came around and was absent from my life. But, as you know by now, grace changes everything!

In the final chapters, I'll share with you my story and how God's grace has, indeed, changed everything for me. My hope is that this same grace will change everything for you as well!

Chapter 13

The Life God Wants For Us

> Then said Jesus to those Jews which believed on him,
> If ye continue in my word, then are ye my disciples
> indeed; And ye shall know the truth, and the truth
> shall make you free. John 8:31-32 KJV

When Jesus came to earth, He came for a purpose. His presence on earth made possible the sacrifice that God required to pay the price for our redemption. *The concept of being found guilty because of who we are, rather than by what we have done, is the basis for the entire gospel.* Humanity is in a sort of quarantine state until the exchange God wants for us takes place in Christ.

Why? For the same reason those who have contagious sicknesses are quarantined in the hospital. We would never dream of exposing healthy people to fatal diseases. The pure and perfect Spirit of God requires a clean slate.

Notice the words of Jesus in the opening passage. He addressed those who believed He was who He said He was. Coming to Christ with our own preconceived notions about Him hides His true nature. When we believe Jesus is who He says He is, He becomes the object of our faith, and we have confidence in His power and grace apart from anything we may or may not do.

When we continue in His word, we stay in step with God. To stay in step with God also means that we are always in a posture of learning. Many believers stumble at this point. As long as we are alive, we are growing and learning. While we are righteous in God's eyes, we must continue to grow in this knowledge of Jesus Christ and His grace.

> Grace and peace be multiplied unto you through
> the knowledge of God, and of Jesus our Lord,
> 2 Peter 1:2 KJV

> But grow in grace, and in the knowledge of our Lord
> and Saviour Jesus Christ. To him be glory both now
> and forever. Amen. 2 Peter 3:18 KJV

Our walk with Christ will be stagnant and uneventful if we fail to realize that, as a disciple, we are on a quest for God's knowledge in this world. God's grace not only saves us, but it also teaches us. When we know the truth, this knowledge of this truth sets us free to live the life God wants for us.

SIN

> For when ye were the servants of sin, ye were free from
> righteousness. What fruit had ye then in those things
> whereof ye are now ashamed? for the end of those things
> is death. But now being made free from sin, and become
> servants to God, ye have your fruit unto holiness, and
> the end everlasting life. Romans 6:20-22 KJV

What do the words "But now being made free from sin" mean to you? If we never realize what Christ has done for us, we will try to do for ourselves what we think needs to be done. The concept of being free from something often escapes us because it is a spiritual reality, which is not often lived in the natural world. Christ placed Himself on

140

the cross and exchanged Himself for our sin. At the resurrection, He made it possible to live a life free from sin because of an exchange in the spiritual world that will make itself known in the natural realm.

> And if Christ be not raised, your faith is vain; ye are yet in your sins. 1 Corinthians 15:17 KJV

Historical records can show us that many have been pronounced dead and, by some miracle, have come back to life, but not in the power of God. In fact, the roots of our modern funeral wake are found in the idea that the person who had passed away might wake up! But Jesus didn't just come back to life in the body He died in; it was a resurrected body that appeared differently to all who met Him after the resurrection. He appeared to Mary, the disciples, and the three on the road to Emmaus, and He wasn't recognized as Jesus.

The cross of Jesus Christ is the turning point for humanity. The Roman cross was the equivalent of our modern day execution chair. It was where those accused of a crime paid the price for that crime. The power of His resurrection is often overshadowed by the tragedy of the cross. Jesus told His disciples that He would go to the cross, but death would not hold Him. His resurrection heralds the dawn of a new time and way we can access the power of God:

> Therefore if any man be in Christ, he is a new creature: old things are passed away; behold, all things are become new. 2 Corinthians 5:17 KJV

The knowledge of our sin serves no purpose other than to hold us in bondage to sin:

> For when ye were the servants of sin, ye were free from righteousness. What fruit had ye then in those things whereof ye are now ashamed? for the end of those things is death. But now being made free from sin, and become servants to God, ye have your fruit unto holiness, and the end everlasting life. Romans 6:20-22 KJV

Take the words from Paul at face value. *Not only are we freed from the consequences of sin, but we are freed from the power sin has in our life.* This isn't a promise that is in the future for us, but a reality in the present. What purpose would it serve the Kingdom if God made those promises only available in the future?

> And all things are of God, who hath reconciled us to himself by Jesus Christ, and hath given to us the ministry of reconciliation; To wit, that God was in Christ, reconciling the world unto himself, not imputing their trespasses unto them; and hath committed unto us the word of reconciliation. Now then we are ambassadors for Christ. 2 Corinthians 5:18-20 KJV

God's plan for His people is for us to share with the world His hope, peace, comfort and power. His grace alone gave us these blessings. When we begin to understand that, by His grace, we have been given new life not by keeping all the rules, we are living like heirs to the Kingdom, not slaves to a system:

> For the law was given by Moses, but grace and truth came by Jesus Christ. John 1:17 KJV

Sin is the great equalizer. Sin puts everyone who has ever lived on the same level. None is better and none is worse. It had to be this way in order for all of humanity to have access to God's grace. Sin is sin. This simple three letter word carries with it condemnation and guilt that will never allow the children of God to live accordingly. As long as we shoulder the guilt of these sins, we will never be those beacons of light God wants. We will, in fact, be putting our lights under a bush. From this position, we view ourselves in a way that God doesn't. *Why would God condemn us with the very same thoughts He died to free us from: guilt, shame, feelings of inadequacy, self-loathing?* If this were the case, then the promises of God are no more than a carrot on a stick: always present, but forever out of reach.

The greatest example we have of a life lived in the grace of God, with the exception of Jesus, is the apostle Paul. Paul called himself the worst of sinners, but in the world of religion, he was second to none.

> Circumcised the eighth day, of the stock of Israel, of the tribe of Benjamin, a Hebrew of the Hebrews; as touching the law, a Pharisee; Concerning zeal, persecuting the church; touching the righteousness which is in the law, blameless. But what things were gain to me, those I counted loss for Christ. Philippians 3:5-7 KJV

We often miss the statement concerning his "righteousness which is in the law." Paul was not only an expert at what the law stated, but in how he lived out the law. His heart was focused on God even when he was persecuting the people who claimed to be followers of the way. His whole life was focused on proving his worthiness to God, but none of that was what God wanted. Instead, Paul was humbled in the presence of the resurrected Christ and received the grace of Jesus. After that, things were never the same. The grace of Jesus Christ changed Paul forever.

It seems appropriate, as we near the end of this book, to finish where we began: with the power of grace.

> Therefore being justified by faith, we have peace with God through our Lord Jesus Christ: By whom also we have access by faith into this grace wherein we stand, and rejoice in hope of the glory of God. Romans 5:1-2 KJV

Our faith in Jesus Christ, not our own actions, made us worthy in God's eyes. From then on, we will be at peace with Him. There is no commuted sentence that we will address at a later date. *From this faith, we are ushered into the grace-filled presence of God, and we stand!* God isn't looking for groveling subjects, but grace filled saints who bring heaven to earth:

> Wherefore, as by one man sin entered into the world, and death by sin; and so death passed upon all men, for that all have sinned: (For until the law sin was in the world: but sin is not imputed when there is no law. Nevertheless death reigned from Adam to Moses, even over them that had not sinned after the similitude of Adam's transgression, who is the figure of him that was to come. But not as the offence, so also is the free gift. For if through the offence of one many be dead, much more the grace of God, and the gift by grace, which is by one man, Jesus Christ, hath abounded unto many. And not as it was by one that sinned, so is the gift: for the judgment was by one to condemnation, but the free gift is of many offences unto justification. For if by one man's offence death reigned by one; much more they which receive abundance of grace and of the gift of righteousness shall reign in life by one, Jesus Christ.) Romans 5:12-17 KJV

If Jesus fulfilled all the requirements of the law, then the law has been fulfilled and sin is not the issue! Read Romans 5:13 again.

> For until the law sin was in the world: but sin is not imputed when there is no law. Romans 5:13 KJV

Paul makes it clear, where there is no law, there is no sin! The power of the resurrection not only frees us from the consequences of sin, but the power of sin in our lives:

> *But by the grace of God I am what I am:* and his grace which was bestowed upon me was not in

vain; but I labored more abundantly than they all: yet not I, but the grace of God which was with me. 1 Corinthians 15:10 KJV (italics mine)

God's grace alone makes us who we are. The things we do count as nothing unless the Spirit of God holds sway in our lives. Our feelings control much of what we do and how we think of ourselves. When we don't feel holy or we don't feel like we deserve the things God promised, understanding who we are apart from how we feel releases us to be who God wants us to be.

The most vivid picture of this in the Bible happened in the Garden of Gethsemane, just before Jesus went to the cross. Jesus didn't "feel" like going to the cross. In fact, He asked God to let Him off the hook, if it was at all possible.

Saying, Father, if thou be willing, remove this cup from me: nevertheless not my will, but thine, be done. Luke 22:42 KJV

What we often overlook is how our responses to God's desires can either hinder His grace or multiply His blessing of grace in our life. When Jesus, in faith, surrendered His will to God, God was true to His word and gave the supply needed:

And there appeared an angel unto him from heaven, strengthening him. Luke 22:43 KJV

Jesus didn't give up, nor did He imply that, since God has control of every situation, my actions don't matter. God won't force His grace on anybody. Those who choose to live by the law will be allowed to do just that. But be aware of the consequences that accompany that decision.

For as many as are of the works of the law are under the curse: for it is written, Cursed is every one that continueth not in all things which are written in the

book of the law to do them. But that no man is justified
by the law in the sight of God, it is evident: for, The
just shall live by faith. Galatians 3:10-11 KJV

If after we have met Christ, we constantly try to hold onto our
place in the kingdom, then through our actions we return to the very
same law from which we were released.

Thou therefore, my son, be strong in the grace that is
in Christ Jesus. 2 Timothy 2:1

Paul encourages His spiritual son, Timothy, to be strong in the
grace of Jesus Christ, not in his own actions or his way of thinking.
When we rightly understand and apply these words of Paul, the Spirit
of God opens up to each of us a new, powerful way of living.

LIFE IN THE SPIRIT

One day, while studying in my office, a member of the church
came for a visit. As he sat across from me, he began to explain his
way of doing things in the church. As the discussion progressed, he
informed me of his non-belief in tithing. At first I was elated. Tithing
was an Old Testament standard that doesn't apply to New Testament
believers. As New Testament believers we are free to give from our
abundance that God has blessed us with. While tithing is a good
starting point, it is not a standard by which we gauge our holiness.

But his stance was that what he had was his and that, because of
the cross, he was alleviated from the burden of giving at all! I was
speechless, to say the least.

*When misunderstood, grace becomes "slippery". But law
when misunderstood is bondage.*

As long as our churches live by the law and not by the Spirit, our
presence and effect in the world will be minimal:

This I say then, Walk in the Spirit, and ye shall not
fulfill the lust of the flesh. For the flesh lusteth against

> the Spirit, and the Spirit against the flesh: and these
> are contrary the one to the other: so that ye cannot do
> the things that ye would. Galatians 5:16-17 KJV

The more I study, pray and ask God about how walking in the Spirit looks, the simpler the answer He reveals. Walking in the Spirit is not a mysterious concept that only the religious elite can attain. It is a promise that all are invited to because of His grace.

Some churches I have visited have been nothing short of a circus, complete with all the eye candy we can handle, while some are worse than many funerals I have been blessed to officiate. When asked, the church leaders claim to be doing things in a Spirit led, holy manner, while other churches who do church differently are held in contempt. This polarized way of presenting God ("our church has it right, others are all wrong") has slammed the door of grace in the faces of those who are earnestly looking for hope.

Walking in the Spirit is nothing short of focusing on who God is first. When we focus our attention on His righteousness, His grace flows freely. When we focus on what we want from Him, we miss the mark.

> But seek ye first the kingdom of God, and *his*
> *righteousness*; and all these things shall be added
> unto you. Matthew 6:33 KJV (italic mine)

If we are telling people what God does, instead of who He is, then we make Him into the image of a vending machine, operated by the actions of saints. No wonder people often reject God. He begins to look a lot like a magic genie rather than a loving God.

> And whatsoever we ask, we receive of him,
> because we keep his commandments, and do those
> things that are pleasing in his sight. And this is his
> commandment, That we should believe on the name
> of his Son Jesus Christ, and love one another, as he

gave us commandment. And he that keepeth his commandments dwelleth in him, and he in him. And hereby we know that he abideth in us, by the Spirit which he hath given us. 1 John 3:22-24 KJV

Notice the lack of commandments and laws in John's writings. In fact, he repeats exactly what Jesus said: "Love God, love people." These two "commandments" are the precursors of walking in the Spirit. The only way to love people in a Godly way is to love God first and then, from His love given to us, we love others.

This I say then, Walk in the Spirit, and ye shall not fulfill the lust of the flesh. Galatians 5:16 KJV

Walking in the Spirit isn't an emotional roller coaster. We don't have to feel a certain way to walk in the Spirit. There are no proper postures or words to speak that ensure the Spirit will fall over us. The presence of His Spirit doesn't always imply that people will fall down or run screaming up and down church aisles. What God does promise is that if we walk in His Spirit, sin will not be an issue! But as long as we insist on doing things by a set of standards that we enforce on ourselves, God's Spirit will be quenched:

But if ye be led of the Spirit, ye are not under the law. Galatians 5:18 KJV

Walking in the Spirit allows the people of God to act like people of God towards one another. Think of it like this: if you and I have an argument and we are both believers, then either the Holy Spirit is fighting against the Holy Spirit, which is impossible, or our flesh is the culprit. If we turn our attention towards God during those times, His Spirit guides our actions and words. During those times, what we experience may not "feel" comfortable; our flesh and Spirit are in a battle.

I'm not, for a moment, implying that sin is eradicated here on earth and that we as people will not sin towards one another. That is impossible as long as we live in a fleshly body. However, the scriptures point us to the actions of the Holy Spirit in our lives that keeps the flesh in check. If we insist on living by a set of standards, then walking in the Spirit will always be just out of our reach:

> Are ye so foolish? having begun in the Spirit, are ye
> now made perfect by the flesh? Galatians 3:3 KJV

The new life God gives us can't be improved upon by continuing to measure our righteousness against the laws. Our standard is Christ alone. Trying to reach perfection by our actions would be like finding a dirty glass in the sink and cleaning only the outside before we drink. Our actions will only clean the outside; God's Spirit takes care of the inside. Grace does indeed change everything.

Chapter 14

Grace-filled Worship

> But the hour cometh, and now is, when the true
> worshippers shall worship the Father in spirit and in
> truth: for the Father seeketh such to worship him. God
> is a Spirit: and they that worship him must worship
> him in spirit and in truth. John 4:23-24 KJV

In the Kingdom of God, worship is an often misunderstood blessing, much like grace, that God desires His people to share. Worship takes many forms in many different churches. But at its core, worship is an opportunity for His people to occupy the same space with others who share the blessing of a new life Christ gave them, united in His Spirit. Unfortunately, the form of worship takes precedent over what real worship is all about. No matter what style of music, spoken word, drama, or testimony, *the motivation to worship comes from a heart overflowing with His grace.*

Understanding what worship is and how God wants us to worship Him has been explained in many different ways by many different people. But from a biblical standpoint, the definition may just rattle us. The Hebrew word for worship means to prostrate oneself or to bow down in reverence. The Greek word actually gives a word picture of a dog licking a master's hand.

Many believers are longing for the Pentecostal experience of the first New Testament service. Pentecost means "fiftieth." It was on this day, the fiftieth day after Passover, that Peter stepped out after the Spirit of God fell on him and gave the first New Testament sermon:

> And when the day of Pentecost was fully come, they were all with one accord in one place. And suddenly there came a sound from heaven as of a rushing mighty wind, and it filled all the house where they were sitting. And there appeared unto them cloven tongues like as of fire, and it sat upon each of them. Acts 2:1-3 KJV

No music, no drama, no special service to usher in the Spirit of God. Peter was moved by the Spirit of God, because of His grace. Afterwards, these people went from house to house ministering to one another:

> Then they that gladly received his word were baptized: and the same day there were added unto them about three thousand souls. And they continued stedfastly in the apostles' doctrine and fellowship, and in breaking of bread, and in prayers. And fear came upon every soul: and many wonders and signs were done by the apostles. And all that believed were together, and had all things common; And sold their possessions and goods, and parted them to all men, as every man had need. And they, continuing daily with one accord in the temple, and breaking bread from house to house, did eat their meat with gladness and singleness of heart. Acts 2:41-45 KJV

This is a far cry from the one hour of worship on Sunday we see in the American church. Granted, our culture is different from that of the New Testament church, but God is still the same God. It's our understanding of what worship truly is that often creates the confusion in churches today. Jesus had a conversation with a woman that had questions about worship that gives us some insight as to what worship is really about.

At the Well

During the hottest part of the day, Jesus rested at a well where those who drew water for household use frequented. Jesus sat alone at the well while His disciples were gathering meat for a meal. It was noon and the well was deserted, except for a lone woman who ventured out in the heat of the day to draw water. As she approached, Jesus struck up a conversation with her which not only changed her life, but the lives of many of the townspeople that day.

It was unusual for someone to be out in the midday heat, as most of the outside chores would have been done during the early morning hours when temperatures were cooler. As the conversation progressed, we read that the woman had been married five times and was living with a man who wasn't her husband:

> The woman answered and said, "I have no husband." Jesus said unto her, Thou hast well said, I have no husband: For thou hast had five husbands; and he whom thou now hast is not thy husband: in that saidst thou truly. John 4:17-18 KJV

This woman, who had come to the well in the middle of the day, probably to escape the scorn of other wives who knew her living arrangements, was caught off guard by the statement Jesus made. So she ventured another question. After all, what would be the harm? If He already knew that she was living in the manner she was (though they had never met), maybe He could provide some insight as to how to properly worship:

Our fathers worshiped in this mountain; and ye say, that in Jerusalem is the place where men ought to worship. John 4:20 KJV

During the reign of King David, God shared with him the vision for the temple and how his son Solomon would build it. The temple was constructed during the reign of Solomon at Jerusalem on Mount Moriah, but after Solomon, the kingdom split. The southern kingdom of Judah retained its place of worship at the temple in Jerusalem, while the northern kingdom of Israel moved its place of worship to a hill in the original city of Samaria. This created quite a stir among the Jewish community who looked at those worshipping and living in the northern kingdom as non-Jews. The mere fact that Jesus, a Jew, was speaking to a woman, a sinful Samarian woman no less, shows us the heart of God. His gospel is for everyone, everywhere:

But the hour cometh, and now is, when the true worshippers shall worship the Father in spirit and in truth: for the Father seeketh such to worship him. God is a Spirit: and they that worship him must worship him in spirit and in truth. John 4:23-24 KJV

Living like God intends us to live not only allows us to walk in the Spirit, but worship Him in Spirit as well. If we have trouble walking in the Spirit, worshipping in the Spirit will be impossible. Walking in the Spirit prompts our worship. What often causes us problems in our worship is the lack of attention to our everyday spiritual life. From a heart changed by the grace of God comes our worship to this awe-inspiring God who meets our every need and gives us the ability to overcome life with all its unpredictable twists and turns.

The Samarian woman, like many of us, equated God with a place. Our churches are not holy ground as the temple was in the days before Christ tore the veil. We don't have to go to a place to worship.

We carry God with us because, as Peter says, "we are living stones," and the same Spirit of God that was in Jesus is in us. Our church buildings are metal, stone or wood, but we, as God's people, bring life to that building as we come together for our corporate worship. As we walk in His Spirit, our worship is not once-a-week, in a certain place proposition. It is a life of continual worship at home, at work, and even at play. When we come together, our worship unites all children of God for a time of fellowship and celebration.

Worshipping God in truth simply means we worship the God who is, not the God we want.

God makes His nature clear in the Bible, but influences from other sources often distract us from His true nature. When we realize the magnitude of His existence and His presence, our natural response in the Spirit will be much like the reception we receive when we arrive home after a long day at work and find our family pet waiting for us. Our pets love us just because we are there. That's God's plan for us: to love Him because He is.

This picture often elicits negative responses from those who think this means we are God's pets. But from the pet's point of view, they don't care; they are just happy their master is with them. Pets don't have pride issues like the human race.

The Jews were chosen by God, not because they deserved it. God doesn't shower us with His love because we deserve it, but because He is a grace filled God who loves His people. His grace changes everything

Epilogue
My Story

I am crucified with Christ: nevertheless I live; yet not
I, but Christ liveth in me: and the life which I now live
in the flesh I live by the faith of the Son of God, who
loved me, and gave himself for me. I do not frustrate
the grace of God: for if righteousness come by the law,
then Christ is dead in vain. Galatians 2:20-21 KJV

Looking back at where I have been on my walk with Christ leaves
me eagerly anticipating the future. What God has revealed to
me during this journey has been nothing short of miraculous. I
remember, during the first year after fully accepting Christ as an
adult, the newness of life and the way He changed my attitude and
outlook. But as time wore on, the newness faded, and what was a
blessing from God now seemed to be much more like work. I began
to meet other believers who were trapped in a way of thinking which
stunted their growth and dimmed their vision of the future. What
I was experiencing was the same emptiness that, twenty years prior,
had derailed my relationship with God.

From an early age, I remember sitting in the church pews
listening to the preacher and saying to myself, "I want that!" But
I didn't know the way to gain access to this life; I just knew that
I wanted it. But there were stunning contradictions in what I saw
the people of God do and what God was telling His people to do.
It wasn't so much the bad actions that caught my attention, but the
bad actions precipitated by a loveless religion. I heard every Sunday

—actually, every day, because I attended a Christian school — about this loving God who, because we couldn't ever seem to get things right, punished missteps with illnesses and natural disasters. And there was always that nagging question of sin. If Christ told me I was forgiven, why were those forgiven sins revisited?

I have already shared the battle of not knowing my father and how this hampered my relationship with a Heavenly Father. What began to emerge is an inconsistent picture of God's nature. Did He really care about me and, if He did, would He punish me when I messed up? What I couldn't understand was if things were sort of ok before Jesus, why would I want to take on a way of life that ensured constant condemnation?

At the age of seventeen, my grandmother died of a massive heart attack. This was the beginning of my downward spiral. My mother loved me and did all she could to ensure I was loved and protected, but parenting is not a single-person proposition. We damage our kids when we insist that we are not fulfilled in our marriages and then leave those relationships for greener pastures. Our kids learn by example that we are somehow meant to live a happy life, and if things get too tough, we have the option of leaving. This was the path my father chose. My hope is that he hears of this book and possibly reads it, but most of all; I want him to know I forgive him and pray he finds grace in the eyes of God.

Not long after my grandmother passed away, my best friend Jeff was killed in a car accident. Jeff was my constant companion growing up and, even today, I miss him dearly. He was actually instrumental in helping me through the loss of my grandmother. Now he was gone and I felt alone. My question to God was, "where are You? If this is life with You, no thanks." Up until that time, honestly I was riding the fence, I went to church and knew God, but I found partying to be a much simpler way of life. The expectations were a lot lower. I could be the life of the party; I couldn't be all the things people told me believers were supposed to be. Besides, from my vantage point, they were all hypocrites, anyway.

Life wasn't exactly panning out how I had planned – actually, it was exactly how I planned because I had no plan – so at the age of nineteen, I joined the United States Air Force.

This wasn't my decision. One day, my step-father came home and informed me that when he came home from work the next day, he would take me to the Marine Corps recruiter. I had no direction, no plan, and it was time to man up. His idea of manning up and mine however, were slightly different. Instead of the Marine Corps I enlisted in the Air Force. Many parents may disagree with the actions of my step-father, but it saved my life.

I thank God for my step-father. He wasn't a believer during my childhood, but he gave me the structure I needed. He was the only real father I ever knew. Some years later, he came to know Jesus, and now both of my parents are actively involved in church ministry. In fact, for a season, they traveled from church to church raising support for a ministry they supported which gave away free Bibles.

About a year after arriving at my permanent duty station, I met the light of my life, Shirley. After a short time of dating, we were married and settled into a life of wedded bliss. At least, that was my expectation. Truth be told, life for us was far from blissful. We fought, I drank, we fought more, and I drank more. About four months after we were married, I found myself in an alcohol treatment facility in Texas. I made it through the thirty-day treatment process and went back to my duty station to resume life. But life never really got any better.

My marriage spiraled out of control, and with it, my drinking habit. During this time, my enlistment in the Air Force came to an end, and I returned to civilian life. Shirley became pregnant with our first son, and she made the decision she would not live with an abusive and unpredictable drunk. She had enough and she packed her clothes and left. Looking back, it was one of my darkest moments.

My unborn child and wife were not with me, and I fooled myself into thinking I was better off without them.

By some miracle, we reconciled and moved to Missouri to begin a new life, but this new life wasn't so new after all. The definition of insanity is doing the same thing and expecting different results. My life was the picture of insanity. During this time, my second son was born, and I felt the pressure of fatherhood. I worked just about every waking hour. Not that we needed that much money, but I needed something to feel good about because I didn't feel good about the life I was giving my family emotionally.

Finally, my wife had enough and again, for the second time, she left with both kids and presented me with an ultimatum: stop drinking or we won't be back. But what I failed to realize was that my drinking problem, along with all my other problems, was a symptom of a much deeper issue. Much like Cain, my need to know I mattered and was valued became the driving force behind the way I lived life. While on the outside my life looked normal, behind closed doors it was far from the ideal scenario.

Over the next couple of years, I managed to keep my drinking somewhat under control, but my attitude stayed the same. It was during this time my wife, desperate for help, received Christ on the way to work one morning while listening to a Christian radio station. She began attending a larger church in the area and would attend every Sunday with both kids. Then as soon as service was over, she would bolt out the doors with the kids in tow and come home to tell me about what she heard the preacher say. My response, however, would always steal away her joy.

During this time, a mutual friend of ours came to visit for a few days. She had recently found hope in Christ and began to share what she was experiencing in her life. One Friday evening, my wife and she rented a popular Christian movie that had been adapted from a popular Christian novel. I wanted nothing to do with it. In fact, I made sure they kept the volume low so as not to disturb me while

I worked on the computer. But one particular scene in particular caught my attention.

A preacher stood before an empty church asking why Christ had returned to take the church and he was left behind. This stopped me in my tracks. No matter what I thought about Christians, I knew that, one day, Christ would return, and I could think of no reason why He would take me. What was worse, I had two sons who were following in my footsteps. I couldn't shake that thought. The following weekend found me in church, and from that time on, things began to change.

One evening, I was in my garage talking things over with God when my wife came down to talk with me. The words she said changed our lives forever. She remembered that, while we were dating, I had shared with her about the time, as a teenager, I had a sense that God wanted me to be a preacher. I didn't understand what that exactly looked like, but the more I sought God, the more unsettled I became. She said, "Kevin, if God wanted you to be a preacher, then maybe He wants that for you now, and if that's the case, you'll never find peace until you do things His way." The conversation we had about this particular subject had not been spoken of for almost twelve years; I had even forgot that I had shared this with her. But I knew she was right. So the next Sunday, I "announced" this news to the church I was attending.

Months passed and, because church life is what it is, chances to actually do ministry were few and far between. As I prayed about what this "call" to ministry looked like, I was informed by my pastor that a church of a different denomination was without a pastor. I jumped at the opportunity and, within weeks, had been "elected" as the new pastor. The pay was negligible, but I didn't care. I was now a bi-vocational pastor. That was one of the greatest seasons of my life, and I thank God for that opportunity.

It was during this time I had a conversation with my supervisor at the garage where I worked and informed him of my new position at church. Keep in mind, I had been employed with this company for several years, so when I received Christ, they noticed a drastic change in my lifestyle and attitude. Then when I started pastoring, they really didn't know what to think!

Unfortunately, my plans and the company's plans didn't mesh. Their plans for me included attending a high level diagnostic class for automotive technicians. This class was expensive and technicians were required to sign a contract to stay employed with this company for a term of eighteen months. If, during that time, the technician opted to leave the company, he or she would have to pay back the tuition for the class. I informed my supervisor that signing a contract would be out of the question because I wasn't sure what my responsibilities at the church would entail. I didn't know how this ministry thing worked. I had no plans at that time to leave, but I needed time to figure out what God was calling me to do. Three days later, I was called into my supervisor's office and informed that my services would no longer be needed. I still remember the look on my supervisor's face when he told me the news. He couldn't believe upper management had made a decision like that. But I was ecstatic! I had actually been praying for God to show me what He wanted me to do, and now He had. I threw myself into the ministry. Incidentally, this company contacted me a few months later and rehired me part-time, earning more money than I was making while working full-time.

This all brings me back to where I started this story at the beginning of this chapter. The longer I was in the ministry, the tougher things got. I naively thought that people who espoused to be Christians would act like Christians. I not only received wounds from others in the ministry, I wounded others. The law and all the commandments were my guiding light. Living by the law gives us the power to inflict harm on others. Soon I was so bound up in legalism that I began to look much like the Pharisees. Life as a believer became hard work. Life as a pastor became impossible; I couldn't live up to the standard of holiness that God demanded, no matter how hard I tried. I resigned from ministry and became a pew sitter. I didn't have what it took to be a pastor; the bar was too high. Not long after I left the ministry, I stopped attending church. I knew that being a pastor differed only in duties as a believer, not standards. The bar would always be high in the kingdom.

The universal weakness of the church is the understanding that God gives us salvation, but not the power to live like redeemed people. In other words, God redeems us, but afterwards, it's up to us. We live by rules and regulations. These rules and regulations are what set us apart from the world, instead of our love for God and His people. Rules and doctrine replace love and grace.

For many churches, their denominational doctrine is their guiding principle. These same church doctrines divide the body, making it weak and ineffective in the world today.

After a long and difficult journey, made worse by errant teaching and legalism that permeates the body of Christ, I found the answer to all of my questions: grace. Now the Bible began to make sense. I no longer read the Bible as a rule book disguised as a love letter. I have heard many people say that the Bible was God's love letter to the world, but those same people teach of a God who scares His people into loving Him. Mess up and condemnation awaits. After all, doesn't God chasten those He loves? The Bible does say God chastens those he loves, but chastening is a far cry from the punishment of God found in natural disaster and plagues. Punishment is for retribution; chastening is for restoration. These same people visit the altar week after week begging for forgiveness already given at the cross. Their prayer always begins, "Lord, forgive us of our sins." The gospel of Jesus Christ, found in the sacred Word of a loving and grace-filled God, emphatically and undeniably tells us He already has! Thank God for grace! Now, because of His grace, I read the Bible in a totally different way.

The best example I have ever heard to explain what I have experienced came from a Sunday morning sermon, and while I don't remember the subject of the sermon, I'll never forget the example. Imagine that your eyesight is bad enough that, in order to read the words on a projector screen, you have to wear glasses. One day, someone comes in and informs you that glasses are not allowed in the room, so in order to read the words on the screen, you'll just have to try harder! So try harder is exactly what you do. You can make out certain letters, but for the most part, things are a massive blur. This seems like an extreme example, but it's not far from what we tell people when we explain the gospel. Life is out of focus and doesn't make sense, so we tell them God is the answer. But in order to live this "blessed" life, we have to try really hard to keep the rules. If we could keep the rules, we wouldn't have needed God in the first place!

Just like the person who wears glasses needs them to see words on a screen, we need assistance to live the life God wants us to live, and trying harder isn't the answer. A person who has trouble seeing words on a screen may concentrate very hard and be able to see a few of the words, but from my experience, it will give you a headache. We may enjoy limited success when we do try harder, but we will wear ourselves out.

While in the second grade, my oldest son was experiencing headaches during class. My wife and I made an appointment with the optometrist and discovered that he required glasses. I'll never forget his response when he first put those glasses on. "Wow, I just thought things were supposed to be blurry."

Many believers are experiencing their walk with God in much the same way as someone that needs glasses. Things appear blurry and out of focus. The gospel they hear contains hints of new life, but is just out of focus. So, they settle for a watered down version of the gospel. The gospel, when viewed through the lens of God's grace, brings into focus the life He wants to give us. Life as a believer should be a joy, filled with hope and peace. What many experience is just the opposite.

It's no wonder the church is losing ground in the world today. We are losing ground because we are losing people. We are losing ground because we have left God out of the equation. Many of the people the church is losing are members of the younger generation. We teach a gospel that doesn't make sense. The Bible is full of promises and stories of people overcoming life, not just getting by. Signs and miracles abounded, but we say those aren't available to the church today. God healed people back then, but not now. Then, in the same breath, we say God doesn't change.

Our mantra is saved by grace, but our actions clearly state, "get it right, or else!" We claim His grace is what saves us, not works, because we'll brag about our righteousness instead of embracing His, and then add a footnote to the gospel that says, "work harder." But when we read about God's grace and fully accept His grace, it can and will change everything. When we understand God doesn't leave us to live this life on our own, but the same Spirit that lives in Jesus lives in us, our outlook on life begins to change. When we understand every single promise God makes in His Word applies to us, we can confidently face the unexpectedness of life. When we understand all we are as believers, is by God's grace and His grace alone, no strings attached, we will truly be free. It's my hope that from this book you find the grace that changes everything. But don't take what I or anyone else has to say about the gospel. Read the gospel for yourself in the Word of God. The Bible is our source; any other book is merely a help, copied from the original.

By grace and through faith we are saved; it's not anything we have done or will do. It's already done at the cross, finalized at the resurrection, and we are sealed by His Spirit. We are released from living in bondage to rules and regulations which were only meant to point us to Christ, not keep us. The laws that once condemned us now become promises. We will keep God first in our life because He is our source of grace, and from His grace comes our hope of glory. The sin that so easily tripped us up now is not an issue because, by His Spirit, we live like kids of the King, not slaves to sin. Forgiveness was applied at the cross for our sin, past, present and future. God doesn't guilt us into obedience; faith prompts this obedience. When this life is over and we give an account for all our deeds, standing before the throne, while those who chose to do things their way kneel, we will hear our God say, "Well done, my good and faithful servant; enter in my Kingdom." This is the grace that changes everything, forever!

Made in the USA
Lexington, KY
19 November 2012